NATURAL CLASSROOM
ASSESSMENT

T 76636

EXPERTS IN ASSESSMENT

SERIES EDITORS
THOMAS R. GUSKEY AND ROBERT J. MARZANO

ISBN 0-7619-7756-2 (7-BOOK PAPER EDITION)
ISBN 0-7619-7757-0 (7-BOOK LIBRARY EDITION)

NATURAL CLASSROOM ASSESSMENT

DESIGNING SEAMLESS INSTRUCTION & ASSESSMENT

JEFFREY K. SMITH
LISA F. SMITH
RICHARD DE LISI

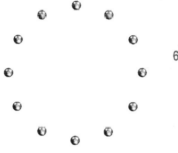

EXPERTS IN ASSESSMENT

SERIES EDITORS
THOMAS R. GUSKEY AND ROBERT J. MARZANO

CORWIN PRESS, INC.
A Sage Publications Company
Thousand Oaks, California

For information:

Corwin Press, Inc.
A Sage Publications Company
2455 Teller Road
Thousand Oaks, California 91320
E-mail: order@corwinpress.com

Sage Publications Ltd.
6 Bonhill Street
London EC2A 4PU
United Kingdom

Sage Publications India Pvt. Ltd.
M-32 Market
Greater Kailash I
New Delhi 110 048 India

Printed in the United States of America

Library of Congress Cataloging-in-Publication Data

Smith, Jeffrey K.
    Natural classroom assessment: Designing seamless instruction and assessment / by Jeffrey K. Smith, Lisa F. Smith, and Richard De Lisi.
        p. cm. — (Experts on assessment kit)
Includes bibliographical references and index.
    ISBN 0-7619-7586-1 (cloth) — ISBN 0-7619-7587-X (pbk.)
 1. Educational tests and measurements—United States—Design and construction. 2. Students—Rating of—United States. 3. Effective teaching—United States. I. Smith, Lisa F. II. De Lisi, Richard. III. Title. IV. Series.
    LB3051 .S586 2000
    371.27—dc21
                                00-008997

This book is printed on acid-free paper.

        01   02   03   04   05   06   7   6   5   4   3   2   1

Editorial Assistant: Catherine Kantor
Production Editor: Diana E. Axelsen
Typesetter/Designer: Rebecca Evans
Cover Designer: Tracy E. Miller

Contents

Series Editors' Introduction

Standards, assessment, accountability, and grading—these are the issues that dominated discussions of education in the 1990s. Today, they are at the center of every modern education reform effort. As educators turn to the task of implementing these reforms, they face a complex array of questions and concerns that little in their background or previous experience has prepared them to address. This series is designed to help in that challenging task.

In selecting the authors, we went to individuals recognized as true experts in the field. The ideas of these scholar-practitioners have already helped shape current discussions of standards, assessment, accountability, and grading. But equally important, their work reflects a deep understanding of the complexities involved in implementation. As they developed their books for this series, we asked them to extend their thinking, to push the edge, and to present new perspectives on what should be done and how to do it. That is precisely what they did. The books they crafted provide not only cutting-edge perspectives but also practical guidelines for successful implementation.

We have several goals for this series. First, that it be used by teachers, school leaders, policy makers, government officials, and all those concerned with these crucial aspects of education reform. Second, that it helps broaden understanding of the complex issues involved in standards, assessment, accountability, and grading. Third, that it leads to more thoughtful policies and programs. Fourth, and most important, that it helps accomplish the basic goal for which all reform initiatives are intended—namely, to enable all students to learn excellently and to gain the many positive benefits of that success.

— *Thomas R. Guskey*
— *Robert J. Marzano*
Series Editors

Preface

This book is written for teachers and those who are about to become teachers. It is about one of the most unpopular topics in education: assessment. Nobody ever got into teaching because they wanted to test students, at least nobody *we* know. In recent years, assessment has gone through something of a revolution, with performance assessment, portfolios, and rubrics working their way into the language of the classroom teacher. As is the case with any new concept or movement within the field, there tends to be more heat than light with regard to these new approaches to assessment. As a classroom teacher, you can be left wondering just what it is you are supposed to do.

How are performance assessments different from what I am currently doing?

How can I develop a good performance assessment?

How should my assessments relate to my instructional goals?

How do I prepare students for assessments?

What should I do about state standards and mandates?

The primary purpose of this book is to provide a practical, commonsense approach to addressing these questions and others. We wrote this book to provide teachers and teachers-in-training with a perspective on assessment that stems from the strengths of good teachers. Instead of starting from the idea of assessment, we start from instruction, and in particular, from the instructional activities that accomplished teachers are so good at developing and executing in the classroom. We don't want you to start with your instructional goals and instructional activities and move from them toward assessment. We believe that assessment that flows logically and closely from instruction will be natural assessment—hence our title, *Natural Classroom Assessment*. Our goal is to take teaching, which we hope you love and feel confident with, and let assessment evolve naturally from it. (We also have a secondary goal: to have this book be entertaining to read by not taking ourselves too seriously and by avoiding the technical jargon of the field.)

Natural Classroom Assessment is written around a series of questions. Each chapter has four or five questions that serve as focal points for the discussion. The book begins with a discussion of instructional goals. Chapter 1 looks at goals by asking the question, What do we want our students to be able to do as a result of being in our classes? In this chapter, we look at classrooms as if they were living organisms into which assessment should function for the good of the whole. Chapter 2 continues this theme by asking how assessment can help or hinder the instructional process based on how it is blended into classroom life. Chapter 3 presents what is really the heart of the issue in *Natural Classroom Assessment*. This is where the idea of developing assessments from classroom instructional activities is explored in depth. Examples are presented that begin with state-mandated instructional goals, then work to instructional activities, and finally to assessments. Chapter 4 completes the basic argument of the text by looking more carefully at how we begin to develop natural assessments.

Chapters 5 through 8 take the idea of developing assessment from instruction and applying it to the major types of assessments those teachers actually use. Chapter 5 looks at performance assessments and projects. Here again, we work from instructional activities and a practical perspective. Chapter 6 looks at that old devil, the multiple-choice test and other forms of objective assessment. Multiple choice can be quite useful; we show you how. Chapter 7 is concerned with crafting essay prompts and report assignments so that these tasks work hand in glove with instructional goals. Chapter 8 examines affective issues in assessment. How do we count participation? Is it fair to grade students based on whether they are working up to potential?

Chapters 9 through 13 discuss a number of critical issues in classroom assessment. Chapter 9 is concerned with preparing students for assessments. This chapter addresses the problem of teaching to the test and getting students to focus on important instructional questions. Chapter 10 examines scoring and communicating results. How to develop rubrics, how to use target essays, and how to set levels of performance are all discussed. Chapter 11 looks at the often-neglected issue of parent-teacher conferences. We have been through these from both sides of the table and have a number of recommendations for making these meetings as productive as possible. Chapter 12 considers special students and inclusion. Here, we look at how to assess special students within the context of regular classroom instruction. Chapter 13 wraps up *Natural Classroom Assessment* and poses the question, Where do we go from here?

Acknowledgments

It's customary to include acknowledgments in the preface of a book. We should begin with our friend and colleague Tom Guskey, who invited us to join in on this effort. Then we would like to thank the teachers who influenced us as we were growing up: Larry Bowers, Richard Hart, Norman Linton, Beth Neiman, Edward Williamson, and Elizabeth E. Zimmerman. Thank you for all of your efforts to teach us to diagram sentences, dissect frogs, discuss novels *en français,* bake a soufflé, and stay on key. We remember it all fondly (well, not the frogs so much) and are inspired by you in our own teaching.

This book is dedicated to our children:

Ben and Leah

Kaitlin

Brian, Michael, and Alex

and is in memory of our friend and colleague, Brenda H. Loyd

About the Authors

Jeffrey K. Smith is Professor of Educational Psychology at Rutgers, The State University of New Jersey, where he has served as Chair of the Educational Psychology department and as Associate Dean of the Graduate School of Education. He teaches courses in statistics, measurement theory, and educational psychology. He conducts research on test performance, grading, learning in museums, and the psychology of aesthetics. In addition to his work at Rutgers, he serves as head of the Office of Research and Evaluation at the Metropolitan Museum of Art. He has written or edited four books and more than 40 articles and has made more than 100 presentations on his research. He has consulted for more than 20 museums and other cultural institutions and more than 30 school districts. He received his PhD from the University of Chicago in 1977 in measurement, evaluation, and statistical analysis.

Lisa F. Smith is Assistant Professor in the Psychology Department of Kean University in Union, New Jersey, where she teaches courses in statistics, measurement, and experimental design. Her research focuses on affective factors that influence test performance, both on standardized tests and in the classroom. She has served as an Academic Advisor on Standardized Testing to the 208th Legislature of the State of New Jersey and was the recipient of the 1999 Emerging Researcher Award sponsored by the American Psychological Association and the New Jersey Psychology Association. She has authored or coauthored more than 30 articles, reviews, monographs, and conference proceedings; four grants; and more than 30 papers at national and international conferences. She has also given 17 invited presentations to groups as varied as sixth-grade gifted students to the Russian and Chinese Ministries of Education. She received her EdD in educational psychology from Rutgers University in 1993.

Richard De Lisi is Professor of Educational Psychology in the Graduate School of Education at Rutgers, The State University in New Brunswick, New Jersey. He joined the faculty in 1976 and is currently Chair of the Department of Educational Psychology and Director of the PhD in Education Program. He offers courses in developmental and educational psychology for preservice teachers and for certified teachers seeking advanced degrees. His areas of special interest are Piaget's theory and sex differences in cognitive abilities. He is currently studying sex differences in advanced mathematical problem solving. He has authored or coauthored more than 40 journal articles, book chapters, and books, including *Moderators of Competence* (1985). He received his PhD in developmental psychology from The Catholic University of America in 1977.

CHAPTER 1

Determining Goals, Targets, and Objectives

What Is the Purpose of This Book?

Natural Classroom Assessment is written for classroom teachers and prospective classroom teachers. Our goal is to provide a different perspective on assessment, one that acknowledges the need for information about how well children are doing, what they are learning, and what their strengths and weaknesses are, and, also, that emanates from the classroom, the instructional goals of the teacher, and the learning goals of the student. We want to make teachers comfortable with developing their own assessments and with evaluating the assessments of others. Our belief is that when assessment is working properly, it is a natural component of the learning and teaching process, not an add-on that intrudes on that process. That's why we decided to call this book *Natural Classroom Assessment*. It reflects our belief that if we put learning first, understand some basic ideas about life in classrooms, and let assessment develop from instruction (not the other way around), we can have assessments that work for instruction and blend into the natural workings of classrooms.

We believe the options for assessment should be wide open. For example, a student has the opportunity to develop organization, research, writing, and editing skills when required to produce a strong paper arguing a position on a topic of current local interest; a teacher then has the opportunity to assess strengths and weaknesses in those areas. Or when a group of students work together to make a presentation on a topic of their own choosing, they have to coordinate their activities, make group decisions, work together as a team, and ensure that all group members are participating. These are strong assessment options. At the same time, a solidly constructed examination accompanied by clear directions to students as to the nature and content of the exam can promote learning and provide clear information on the progress of students.

We have developed this book around a series of questions. This seemed appropriate for a book on assessment. To begin, asking questions is a natural part of assessment; questions engender thinking, contemplation, speculation, the proposition of possible answers. As you read *Natural Classroom Assessment*, we want you to think for yourself about the questions that are posed. In fact, an excellent idea would be to take a minute to think about how *you* would answer the questions, as you come across them, that begin each section in the book. Then see what we have to say about the issue and how that fits with your opinion. We would love to be able to talk with you about various options and points of view, but that's not possible within the confines of the written word. So we have to leave the conversation up to you, but we'll try to consider different possibilities, and we'll try to have a dialogue in spirit, if not in actuality. We begin with what we believe is the most fundamental issue that faces us as teachers.

What Is It That We Would Truly Like Our Students to Be Able to Do?

In thinking about assessment, we started with the notion of what we would like our students to be able to do. This seemed a natural place to start, perhaps even an obvious one. The more we thought about it, the more important the idea became to us. It's a fairly simple notion, but one we think is occasionally overlooked, especially in an era of state mandates on what is to be taught and learned. Take a minute to imagine what you might be able to accomplish with students if you could free yourself of the constraints that exist in the real world of education. Think only about what might be possible in working with the students you have. What would you hope for in terms of how much knowledge they might gain, what habits of mind they might develop over the course of the year, how they might approach problem solving, how they might change what they feel are their personal aspirations? Don't think about your goals in terms of assessment, think about them in terms of what you want to accomplish and how it might affect your teaching. We'll worry about assessment later.

"Now," you might be thinking, "what would be the purpose of this exercise? Much of what I will be teaching has been determined elsewhere by some other individuals or bodies." True enough, but that doesn't mean that you can't contemplate what you think would be important for your students. You may also find that some of the goals you have for students are not inconsistent with those the district has. If you don't articulate what you believe is important for your students, it would be hard to determine at any point in time whether you seem to be working toward those goals or against them. Think of approaching the situation this way: Look at what you are given to work with from whatever level gives it, then look at your goals. Now do your best to reconcile the two and come up with a working definition of what you are trying to accomplish. For example, if you are teaching fifth-grade literacy, you may be presented with a goal from the district that students acquire a certain number of vocabulary words—the words may even be specified. You, on the other hand, may have the somewhat broader and more useful goal of having your students develop the habit of mind to investigate words they come upon that they don't know. Yours and the district's are not the same goals in this case, but they are goals that can be brought together for instructional purposes. The district's goal can be used as the material for development of the broader goal you have in mind.

We grew up in the days of educational objectives; in fact, the lead author of this book is a student of Benjamin Bloom, whose *Taxonomy of Educational Objectives* (Bloom, Engelhart, Frost, Hill, & Krathwohl, 1956) has for decades dominated the discussion of how to establish what students should learn. The concept of educational objectives has gone through any number of metamorphoses, not all of them particularly positive. The problem we saw with objectives is that people got carried away with them. We started seeing objectives along the lines of "Given a number two pencil and a piece of goldenrod paper, the 8- to 9-year-old student will calculate two digit sums with carrying on 20 arithmetic problems with 80% accuracy in a total of two minutes" and "The student will read, in one minute, a 100-word passage with a Dale-Chall readability index of 6.0 to 7.0 with two vocabulary words unknown to the student and will correctly answer at least four of six comprehension questions including two containing the unknown vocabulary words." At the other end of the spectrum, we saw objectives like "Students will explore experiences that they define as meaningful to them in terms of their relationship to the environment."

Our notion here is simple. What would we like students to be able to do at the end of the year (or course of study)? Call it an objective, a target, a goal, a desideratum, it doesn't really matter. State it simply in terms of what a student will be able to do. Forget the percentages and the conditions. You are teaching children, not running rats through a maze. But even though the statement should be simple, the idea doesn't have to be. Broadly stated goals are what we are looking for as guides for instruction. With a half dozen or so well-stated, broad goals for your class or course, you will have an excellent touchstone for considering your instructional activities and, consequentially, for your assessment activities. If this seems a difficult task, or if you are a relatively new teacher, collaborate. Share your ideas with a colleague, ask her to offer a critique or suggestions for improvement. One of the nicest aspects of being in the teaching profession is the willingness of good colleagues to share expertise.

Before leaving the topic of goals and objectives, let us return for a moment to the taxonomy developed by Bloom and his colleagues. The contribution of the taxonomy was twofold: first, to get educators to consider then communicate what it was that they were working toward; second, by highlighting the higher levels of the taxonomy, to encourage educators to consider objectives that existed above the level of accumulation of knowledge. Bloom, who developed the taxonomy to be used at the college level, was concerned that too many instructors were focusing too much effort on the acquisition of knowledge and not enough on concepts like analytical thinking, synthesis, and evaluation. His taxonomy was developed to allow educators to classify their objectives as to what type of mental process would be involved. The taxonomy is hierarchical in nature—knowledge is the most basic level, followed by comprehension, application, analysis, synthesis, and evaluation. Bloom's concern that there not be an overemphasis on knowledge acquisition to the detriment of higher-order thinking skills was well-taken, but we would provide a second perspective on the issue, from about four decades after this taxonomy was developed. Simply stated, there is nothing wrong with knowledge. We get a little nervous when educators put the word *mere* in front of the word *knowledge*. We typically find that people who have a lot of knowledge are pretty well educated, or are considered to be so, and that the reverse is true of people who have little knowledge.

In fact, an anecdote fits well here. One of the authors knew a boy who at age seven could name all of the countries on the globe. You could give him the name of a country and ask him to find it, or you could ask him the name of a country to which you pointed. He acquired the knowledge through his fascination with a globe that he had. For our purposes here, the question is, "Is this useful information to have, or does it fall into the category of 'mere' knowledge?" "Mere" knowledge or not, it is knowledge we would like to have, even though we are well past the age of seven. Armed with that knowledge, this boy would be able to pinpoint geographically any location he reads about. Not bad knowledge to have. And that is just one area in which such knowledge enhances experience.

To sum up, we think that it is critical to start our examination of assessment by determining what we want our students to learn. We recommend keeping to a short list of well-articulated and well-considered goals for our students—goals that could be readily explained and appreciated by other teachers, students, and parents. If we know where we want to go, it will be easier to determine how close we are to getting there.

What Do We Do in Classrooms to Enhance Learning, Development, and Growth?

One of the things that always impresses us in looking at classrooms is the incredible ingenuity and creativity of good classroom teachers. Challenging tasks, group projects, innovative approaches to subject matter, and the opportunity to let students be creative are all hallmarks of the kind of teaching to which we aspire. In developing these activities, a variety of sources and inspirations play a part, including using tried and true activities, borrowing from colleagues, picking up ideas in college courses and workshops, and the simple hard work of thinking about what we want children to be able to do and how we can provide experiences that will get them there. Glatthorn (1998) talks about the concept of assessment-driven instruction. He talks about teaching that is based on the concept of developing performance assessments from standards-based curricula, then teaching to the performance assessments. Although this is similar to what we are talking about here, it is different in some important aspects. We are encouraging the development of strong instructional practices and activities that are derived from the instructional goals, with the development of assessments then being based on the nature of the instruction. We feel that teachers often excel in the development of good instruction, but they do not necessarily also excel in the development of good assessment. We want you to start with instruction, then move to assessment.

An instructional activity obtains its justification from the degree to which it helps students learn, grow, and develop. In evaluating the quality of an instructional activity, look at what it is going to do for the students who will be participating in it. What will the activity require of students? What will it give them the opportunity to do? Might there be different approaches to working on the activity? How will this activity relate to your goals for the students in this class?

At the heart of our recommendations for developing classroom assessments is that you approach it in the same way you would approach developing classroom instructional activities. In fact, we are going to suggest that they be the same thing—that your assessment activities can, in some cases, be the same activity as the instructional activity. In other cases, we will recommend that assessment activities be developed independently of instructional activities, but that they use the same type of logic and development process as the instructional activities.

How Can We Align Our Assessment Activities With Our Instructional Goals?

We are told by friends of ours who are biologists that brine shrimp will always travel toward a light source (they also gave us the name of a microscopic animal that will do the same thing, but we keep forgetting it). Well, students are with activities that affect grades the way brine shrimp are with those light

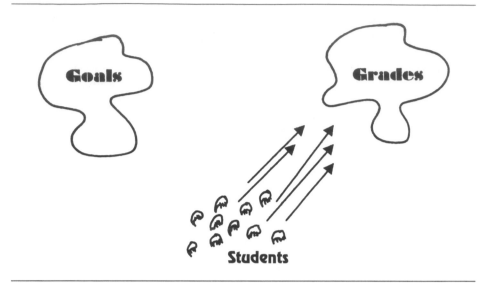

Figure 1.1. What Naturally Attracts Students

sources—that is where the students will put their energy. Whatever results in a grade is what students will attend to (in addition, of course, to the attention they pay to dating, antagonizing the teacher, etc.). As much as we would like them to gravitate toward our instructional goals, students are intentional beings and will do what they perceive to be in their best interest, which, generally, is getting good grades. The situation in which we find ourselves is depicted in Figure 1.1. Needless to say, this is not an optimal situation. What we want to do is to have students work toward the goals of the class. The solution here is straightforward. What we have to do is to ensure that the goals of the class and the assessments in the class are aligned, as in Figure 1.2.

If we align our class assessments with our class goals, then when students work toward one, they will naturally be working toward the other. What does this require on our part as teachers? It requires making sure that the assessments we develop reflect the goals of the class. This requires serious examination of our assessment activities to see exactly what they are requiring of students, how we are grading them, and how we are providing feedback to students so that the assessments and the goals align. If our instructional activities align with our goals as well, it seems reasonable that goals, instructional activities, and assessment activities will be in synch. A caution on this before we move on: If we do not align our grading and assessment activities with our instructional goals, then our instructional goals will become aligned with our grading and assessment activities. By this we mean that the assessment and grading activities will become, de facto, the instructional goals because that is where students will put their efforts. Get the goals first, then build the assessments to reflect them.

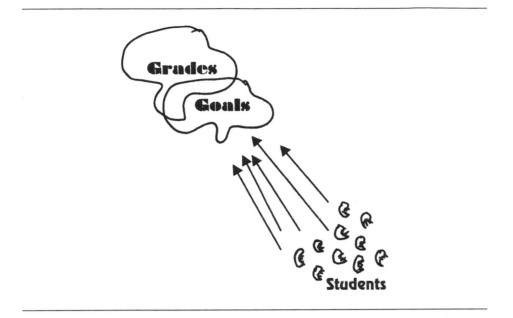

Figure 1.2. Aligning Grades and Goals

How Do Assessment Activities Fit With the Organic Nature of the Classroom?

One might think of a classroom as a living organism. It's a nice metaphor, actually. The classroom is bounded in space and time and contains within it a number of relatively autonomous components that interact with one another in a mostly purposeful fashion. Friends of ours have likened a classroom to a local environment, but we prefer to think of it more as a single-celled creature. OK, a very large single-celled creature (see Figure 1.3).

Different parts of the cell are responsible for different activities, and what affects one aspect or component of the cell affects the rest of the cell. Think of classes you have had in the past—they have collective personalities. You can think of a class that you particularly enjoyed working with or another that was particularly challenging. Each member of the class makes a contribution to that personality, as do the activities that occur in the class. The assessment activities of the class are such a component. When there is an assessment activity or assignment for the class, it becomes an important aspect of the organism. In many respects it becomes the goal of the organism. This can work to the benefit or detriment of the class as a whole. It is important to consider how assessment activities will affect the workings of a class.

When students are working together studying for an exam—perhaps getting together after class to study—then the effect is positive. If they are actively competing with one another for the best grade, the effect is not likely to be

Figure 1.3. The Classroom as a Single Cell Environment

positive. If their group project engenders a spirit of cooperation and creativity, the effect is positive. If it engenders feelings of jealousy or a sense that some members are coasting and relying on others to do the work, the effect will be negative. The question here is, "How will this assessment affect the workings of this class—what will the students do to complete this assessment?" The goal is to keep the class together—working together, achieving goals together, and growing as an organism. Assessments can be viewed as intrusions on the workings of a class, necessary evils that are imposed on the instructional process, or they can be viewed as tasks that challenge the class to attain its potential. Part of the difference between the two possibilities has to do with the nature of the assessments, and part has to do with how the assessments are presented to the students by you, the teacher.

Let's see where we are at the end of this introductory chapter. We want to look at assessment in a new perspective, in a different light. We want to examine, or reexamine, the idea of what our goals are for the class. We want to think about our assessment activities and how they align with our goals. We want to think about how assessments fit into the ecology of our classrooms. We want our assessment activities to be a positive influence on classroom life—to be seen as challenges that help students achieve their potential, that encourage peer relationships, and that build an appreciation for the subjects be-ing studied.

     If all of this sounds like the assessment activities of the classroom would not be all that different from the instructional activities in the classroom, then you've gotten the message of our introduction. We want to argue for an ap-proach to the development of assessments that emanate from an instructional perspective, that grow out of your expertise as a teacher. Let's see where that leads us.

CHAPTER 2

How Will Assessment Be Used?

Do We Really Need to Assess at All?

The authors of this book have more than 50 years of experience (combined) working with schoolteachers. In all of our interactions with teachers, we have never come across one who said, "I got into teaching because I really like giving students tests and grading them." As teachers, we are naturally the advocates of our students. If a student is having a problem understanding something, it is our natural tendency to help the student. Now, the nature of that help might range from "Let me walk through this with you again" to "Where exactly do you think the problem is?" to "I think if you just stay with this a little bit longer, you'll find that you really know how to do it." But whatever approach to assistance we choose, it is based on our judgment as to what is best for the student.

Our role fundamentally changes, however, when we engage in assessment of students. We no longer seem to be acting as the student's advocate, but as the student's judge. We mark test questions as right or wrong, evaluate papers for strengths and weaknesses, judge projects and performances according to the rubrics we have developed for grading. Most of us recognize this as an important aspect of teaching, but it doesn't feel as good as working with the students directly. It can be particularly disturbing when we have to assign grades and when some students are struggling.

Let's revisit the roles of being the advocate of the student and the evaluator of the student. If we take a new perspective on them, we may come to the realization that they are not so different from one another. Think about working with one student on a single learning task. In many respects this provides an optimal learning situation. Think about what options are available to you as the instructor of the student. Here is a list of 20 instructional moves you can make when working with an individual student:

1. Explain to the student what it is the student is trying to learn.

2. Provide the student with an example of what you are talking about.

3. Relate the task to prior learnings of the student.

4. Use a metaphor that you think the student will appreciate.

5. Present a counterexample, something that is similar to what is being learned, but is not correct in some important fashion.

6. You might watch the student try to solve a problem that would demonstrate understanding.

7. Ask the student a question about the task at hand.

8. You can ask the student to try to explain the task to another person.

9. Break the task down into components and present the components to the student in turn.

10. Watch the student's facial expressions as he or she works on the task.

11. Have the student ask you questions about the task.

12. Have the student relate what he or she is learning to other things the student knows or can do.

13. Have the student relate the task to personal experience.

14. Extend what the student is doing into new areas.

15. Decide it is time to stop working on this task at this time.

16. Have the student practice his or her skills.

17. Ask the student to assess his or her learning.

18. Have the student work on skills without your being present.

19. Ask the student how he or she feels about the task.

20. Ask the student to talk through his or her approach to solving the problem.

This is clearly not an exhaustive list. As a teacher you are probably saying, "Wait a minute, these people completely ignored this aspect or that component of working with individual students." We hope you would be able to match our list item for item with ideas based on your own experience. If we were developing this list jointly with you, we would want to hear your ideas. In fact, we would probably hold a number of these instructional moves in abeyance to see what you would come up with. We'd love it if you would take a few minutes right now and develop a short list of your own. Go ahead, give it a try. Really.

Either you did or you didn't come up with a list, but we have to move on, because, well, because this is a book. Now, let's go back and look at our list and look at your list. Do these instructional moves seem reasonable to do when working with an individual student? We like to think so and hope you do, too. Now, go through our list and your list and see if any of the items might reasonably be classified as assessment. Did you guess this was where we were heading? We thought you might. On our list, we see Items 6, 7, 8, 10, 17, 19, and 20 as being clearly related to assessment and Items 3, 4, 11, 12, 13, and 15 as being at least indirectly related to assessment. Although when working with a particular student on a particular task, you surely wouldn't do all 20 of our items, you would probably do many of them and you would almost assuredly do some of those that were listed as assessment. Here's the point: Assessment *is* part of instruction. It's not an add-on, it's not a necessary evil, it's not a nuisance that we wish we could avoid, it's part and parcel of teaching. Excuse us while we take a second to emphasize this point.

> Assessment *is* part of instruction.

So how did assessment get to be so objectionable? We're not sure. It was already there when we went to school.

Now let's change the setting a little. Earlier we said that working one-on-one with a student is in many respects the optimal instructional setting. We hope that some of you might have thought at that point, "Not necessarily. There are some things that I want students to learn that I think can be offered much better in a small group where the students can interact with one another." We agree. In fact, one of us did a study on it (Morrow & Smith, 1990). We found that when reading stories to young children, they tend to become more involved in the story and are better able to retell the story when it is read to them in groups of three than when it is read one-on-one. This is not to say that small-group learning is better than individual learning or the other way around, but that different things happen in different settings.

Some of the items in the list above are more difficult for groups, even groups as small as three, than for individuals. Other items are easier for a group, and some items have the same degree of difficulty regardless of the setting. There are even some items that simply cannot be done by a single student, that can only be done by a group of students.

Items that would be more difficult to do in a group include relating the task to the students' prior learnings (Item 3), because you would have several different sets of prior learnings; watching a student solve a problem (Item 6) because it would be necessary to divide your attention among students; and making a decision as to whether to move on (Items 15 and 20), which would involve consideration of a number of different levels of mastery with respect to the task.

Items that work better with a small group of students include asking a student to explain the task to another student (Item 8), since other students will be right at hand, and having students ask you questions (Item 11). One of the clear findings in research we conducted comparing group to individual story reading was that the group structure facilitated communication. All students asked more questions in the small group structure than in the individual structure. In fact, they fed off one another's questions. Having students relate their learning to other things they know or can do (Item 12) or to their own experiences (Item 13) would also probably facilitate communication.

It seemed to us that most of the remaining items would be fairly similar under these two conditions. However, this, too, is something that you might want to check for yourself. Now we might consider additional items that can only be accomplished in a group structure. Holding a discussion among peers, having one student tutor another on the task, and having the students work together on a group project are just a few of the possibilities. We could come up with quite a few more, but as this is not a book on cooperative learning, we will leave that to you (or people who know a lot more about cooperative learning than we do).

There is one more group we need to consider before moving on: classrooms full of students. As teachers (OK, college professors in our case, which we know is substantially easier than teaching, say, fifth grade), we don't get the opportunity to work one-on-one with students, or even in groups of three. Classes of 15 to 30 students are the norm for kindergarten through 12th-grade teaching. We can sometimes structure the work to get a small-group opportunity, but most of the time we are working with larger groups. We return again to the list of teaching moves to see what becomes easier, more difficult, or remains the same. In the whole class setting, almost nothing is easier. We found that maybe explaining the task to another person (Item 8) might be easier, again because there are other people present. We see explanation (Item 1) as about equally difficult, along with providing examples (Item 2), counterexamples (Item 5), breaking the task down (Item 9), having the student ask you questions (Item 11), having the student relate the task to personal experiences (Item 13), having the student practice (Item 16), and having the student work on skills without you being present (Item 18). Everything else gets harder when the numbers get bigger. By the way, in the study on storytelling mentioned earlier, when we moved from groups of three to whole class storytelling, the group benefit disappeared. In fact, whole class storytelling is not as effective as one-on-one.

Relating tasks to prior learnings (Item 3) and using metaphors (Item 4) become more difficult because prior learnings are different for different learners and a particular metaphor may work well for one student and not for another. Asking the student a question (Item 7) becomes much more difficult when you have 20 students than when you have one or three. How difficult the question should be, whom you should ask, how much you should probe a given response—these are much more complicated when you have to take the learning of 20 students into consideration. Watching students work on a task (Item 6) or watching facial expressions (Item 10) also becomes much more of a challenge as the class size increases. Asking the student how he or she feels about the task (Item 19) or to assess his or her own learning (Item 17) is simple with one student, but not with a large group. And finally, deciding to move on (Items 15 and 20) is a much more difficult decision when it has an impact on a group of people instead of on a single individual.

None of this is telling you anything you didn't know. Teaching 20 is harder than teaching one. Teaching three or four may be optimal for some things, but 20 is better than three for having a chorus or getting a good softball game together. What we want to point out here is that groups particularly exacerbate the problems associated with assessment.

What Is the Underlying Purpose of Assessment in Instruction?

The underlying purpose of assessment in instruction is to assist the instructional process. It's as simple as that. If an assessment is not helping us in doing instruction, it is not being useful. We have to point out, however, that people use assessment for a variety of purposes other than assessment and those purposes may be valid. However, they take us away from the thrust of this book and make things complicated. Assessment gets complicated when we want to use it for purposes other than instruction, such as accountability, program evaluation, grading, merit pay, selection into special programs, college admissions, and a host of other issues. Of the list of alternative uses of assessment, we are only going to touch on one in this book, and that is grading. We will visit the others just briefly in the next section, then let them go. Why? Because this book is called *Natural Classroom Assessment*, not *Natural Classroom Assessment and a Host of Other Issues Only Tangentially Related to Instruction.*

Who Are the Legitimate Audiences for Assessment Results?

There is actually a pretty wide variety of audiences for assessment results, but these audiences are typically not directly interested in instruction. They may be interested in the outcomes of instruction, but not in the instructional process itself. The standards movement is a classic example of this. The fundamental notion of the standards movement in education is something like this: "We'll say what is to be learned, when it is to be learned, how much is to be learned, and what acceptable performance is; then we will leave the accomplishment of the goals we have set to the teachers, because, after all, we wouldn't want to intrude on the instructional process." Frequently, standards

Figure 2.1.

advocates are firm believers that the solution to most educational problems is to set the standards higher. High standards are good, higher standards are better. How we get there is typically not their concern. The position this can put teachers and students in what might be likened to being a high jumper on the high school track team. If Marvin can't jump over the bar when it's set at 5 feet, 6 inches, the obvious solution is to raise the bar to 6 feet. If he fails at 6 feet—you got it—raise it to 7 feet (see Figure 2.1).

Other people in education are interested in assessment because they want to see how well things are working in general; still other groups want to be able to identify students for special purposes, such as remediation, selection into gifted programs, or admission into college. Here are some of these other uses for assessment information.

Audience	Assessment Need
Community	How well is our school (school district) doing?
School administrators	Who should be classified for various instructional purposes?
State school officials	How well are the state and the districts within the state doing?
College admissions officers	Which students are most likely to do well in our college?
Politicians	How does our state compare to others and how does the United States stack up internationally?

These are not illegitimate needs. They simply are not instructional needs, certainly not classroom instructional needs. A variety of issues and problems arise in assessments that are conducted for these purposes, but they are not our concern here.

How Can Assessment Help or Hinder the Instructional Process?

In considering how assessment can help the instructional process, let's start with an everyday example. The other day, a friend called and asked for directions for driving into New York City. Since one of the authors does that on a regular basis (confirming your suspicion that we weren't quite right to begin with because we grew up to be measurement specialists), he agreed to provide help. The conversation went about like this (see page 17).

Lots of instruction, lots of assessment and feedback, comprehension checks, and so on. The fundamental nature of assessment is to let the teacher and the learner know how well the learner is comprehending the material being taught. Jane starts by determining that Jeff is someone she wants to get directions from (your typical fourth-grader will pretty much assume that the teacher is supposed to be the teacher). Next, Jeff moves to establish the goal of the instruction (getting to 48th and Second). Then, assuming that all New Jerseyans know all of the exits of the New Jersey Turnpike and how to get to them, he overestimates Jane's prior knowledge by jumping right to exit 16E off the turnpike. Jane provides the corrective feedback, and Jeff modifies his instructional approach, not only in terms of backing up to how to get on the turnpike but also in his overall assessment of Jane's navigational background

---

Interaction on Giving Directions

Caller (Jane)   Jeff, you drive into the city a lot, right?

Jeff   Yep, two days a week.

Jane   Can you give me directions? I need to go in next week.

Jeff   Sure. Where are you going?

Jane   48th and 2nd.

Jeff   Easy. You're going to take the Lincoln Tunnel off of 16E.

Jane   What's the best entrance onto the turnpike?

Jeff   Where are you coming from?

Jane   Route 1.

Jeff   Use the exit 9 entrance off of 18.

Jane   OK.

Jeff   To get to 16E, you need to take the eastern spur of the turnpike.

Jane   Where does it split?

Jeff   Right around Newark Airport.

Jane   Is it easy to see?

Jeff   It actually is if you are looking for it, but if you miss it, just take 16W and head east on 3. Now when you get off at 16E, stay right and it will put you on the road that leads right to the tunnel. Just don't get off of that road and it takes you right to the helix. Was that too much at once?

Jane   No, but give me a second to write it down.

(pause)

Jeff   Ready?

Jane   Go.

Jeff   OK, when you come out of the tunnel, take the 42nd Street and North exit, which will dead-end you into 42nd, and then you turn right. Take that over to 2nd and turn left. Take that up to 48th.

Jane   I think I've got it. Let me read this back to you to see if it's correct.

---

and savvy. He moves to a more explicit instructional style and makes more frequent assessments as a result of this information. When he picks up the pace near the end, he catches himself and asks Jane how she's doing: "Was that too much?" Jane, who possesses a good deal of knowledge about her learning style, asks for time to make sure she has the material written down, then at the end decides on a final comprehension check: "Let me read this back to you to see if it's correct."

Basically, that's how assessment works to help instruction. It provides both general and specific feedback and suggests corrective measures.

Let's bring this to a classroom setting. Imagine 20 sixth-grade students all driving individually into New York City. Pretty scary thought, huh? Some will end up in Queens, others in Philadelphia, some won't make it out of the driveway. Well, we aren't recommending that 11-year-olds drive cars, and navigating to New York City is not on the scope and sequence chart of many sixth-grade instructional programs, but let's stay with the metaphor for a minute. Let's say that instead of trying to get to 48th and Second, the instructional goal (or what Stiggins, 1991, calls the "achievement target") is to get students to understand what foreshadowing is in literature. We want them to comprehend the concept and be able to find it in the novels they are currently reading. Keeping with our driving instruction metaphor, they have to get in their "literature cars," drive to the comprehension of the concept, then cruise about until they find examples of foreshadowing in the novels that they chose from a list of novels you developed. Your job is to keep them from looking like the bumper car ride has just started up at the local amusement park.

What are you going to do? There are a host of instructional alternatives available to you. You can start with a particularly striking example of foreshadowing so that the students have a touchstone to return to if they get "lost" (confused). You can provide a very clear explanation of what foreshadowing is. You can give them an example of foreshadowing, then ask them to talk about it in groups and share their conclusions. You can give them three brief passages and ask them to pick the passage that uses foreshadowing. You can ask them to think of examples of foreshadowing in the literature that you have read to date as a class. You can have them write a story and put foreshadowing in it, or have them go back to a story they wrote before and add foreshadowing to it.

A question: Which of these activities are instructional and which are assessment? We hope you would agree that most of them are a little of both. Most of them serve the dual role of moving the children ahead a little while at the same time providing the information necessary to see that they are on the right track. We don't let anybody go too long without checking; we don't want anybody spinning out of control. At the same time, we know that instructional progress takes primacy here. We don't want people to spend so much time checking in that they don't make any progress. Assessments that facilitate instruction directly in addition to providing feedback on where students are seem to be particularly useful.

The question that headed this section asked how assessment can be harmful in addition to helpful. Think about that for a minute or two. Can you come up with any examples of assessment being harmful? We thought so. But now eliminate externally imposed assessments that were designed primarily to meet accountability needs. Think of assessment activities of your own doing that might not have helped the instructional process. Any examples here? We think they might crop up in the following situations. First, if you engage in too much assessment, or too little, it can hurt instruction. If you assess too much, you waste time and you can lead your students to believe that the assessments are the goal rather than a means to achieving the goal. Wait—write that down. That's a good point. *Assessment isn't the goal; it's a means to achieving the goal.* Hang on, we'll make it big for better emphasis.

> ## Assessment isn't the goal; it's a means to achieving the goal.

Another way assessment can be harmful is if it's off target. As teachers, we probably run into this more than we would like to think. We're going to address this issue quite specifically a little later in the book, but for now what we are talking about is a lack of fit between the instructional goal and the nature or content of the assessment. If we are interested in foreshadowing, but we ask students to work on figurative language in the same assignment as the foreshadowing exercise, we are taking them off the task. If we are interested in students learning how to estimate answers in mathematics, then make them work out all of the problems exactly, we are diluting their efforts. The best example of being off target that we have come across recently was a high school class that was reading *The Scarlet Letter.* An assignment that counted for 25% of the grade for *the entire marking period in English* consisted of having the students make a scarlet "A." We are not kidding. How did that task relate to instruction? What purpose did it serve? Was it fair to students who were not artistically inclined? We don't object to the assignment as a way to have some fun in the class. We wouldn't object to having it contribute to the participation component of the grade in the class (in a small way) or have it count as extra credit, but surely there is more to *The Scarlet Letter* that is worthy of students' time.

"Joan's appreciation for the mores of 18th-century New England is well developed for a ninth-grader, but, unfortunately, her concept of the cross-stitch . . . " Well, you get the point.

So what are we leaving with? Assessment is not so evil after all, and it doesn't look too different from what I already do in my classroom. It helps me and my students make sure we are headed where we want to go and gives us an idea of how far along we are. It makes us better human beings and enhances the social order. OK, we're pushing it.

CHAPTER **3**

Designing Assessments That Evolve From Instruction

What Is the Basis for Calling a Classroom Assessment "Natural"?

The revolution in assessment that has occurred in the past 10 years has generated a lot of new names for assessment. These include *alternative assessment, authentic assessment, performance assessment,* and *portfolio assessment. Alternative assessment* is the term used to denote an alternative to standard assessment techniques, including multiple choice, probably the most notable of standard assessment techniques. *Portfolio assessment* refers to the collection of a student's work, sometimes the student's best work, sometimes a historical record, sometimes a series of products specifically designed to assess certain abilities or characteristics. *Performance assessment* refers to the student actually producing something in response to a prompt of some kind. *Authentic assessment* has to do with assessment activities that are centered around something meaningful to the child, such as an interview with a grandparent or a story in which the hero is the child's pet. There are a host of publications that relate to this new conceptualization of assessment. Here are a few you might want to look at: Stiggins (1991); Johnson (1996a, 1996b); Wiggins (1996); Linn, Baker, and Dunbar (1991); Danielson and Marquez (1998); Hill and Ruptic (1994); and Rhodes (1993).

In this book, we have chosen to introduce a new term, *natural classroom assessment.* Our idea is probably closest to the notion of authentic assessment, but we feel there are important differences. We think that classroom instruction ought to be the logical source for classroom assessment. Recently there has been a dichotomy set up in educational literature that pits teacher-centered instruction against student-centered instruction. We believe this is a false dichotomy. Instead, we propose that teachers and students work together in classrooms. They each have roles and they come together to form communities called classrooms. As we mentioned before, we think of classrooms as living environments, living organisms, and we believe assessment plays an important function in the roles of these organisms.

The needs, desires, and natural interests of students should play an important role in classroom life; so too, should the knowledge, experience, and wisdom of the teacher. We have always wanted the best teachers for our children for a reason. They know how to build environments in which students can thrive; they know what children learn best and are most ready to learn in their grades; and they know the subject matter they are assigned to teach. Our children don't know any of this. They're children. Therefore, although we like the notion of assessment that takes into account the natural learning interests of the child, as children they don't understand what will be required of them in adult life; this understanding is the responsibility of adults. In particular, it is the responsibility of parents, boards of education, administrators, and, when you actually get right down to it, teachers.

Thus, we look for assessment that facilitates the teaching/learning process in the classroom in which it exists. This is the type of assessment that we call natural classroom assessment. The justification, rationale, and ultimate evaluation of natural classroom assessment is the degree to which it enhances the achievement of the instructional goals for the class in which it is being used. To judge the utility of any given assessment, it is critical to know the instruction to which it is related. Let us provide two divergent examples of this.

Setting 1

First-Grade Literacy

Consider a first-grade classroom in a middle-class school district. Two of the instructional goals for literacy instruction are to improve basic reading skills and to develop a love for reading. These seem reasonable and complimentary goals for a first-grade classroom and leave a fair amount of room on the issue of how to accomplish them. The teacher in the classroom takes a balanced approach to literacy instruction, using some phonics skills, some whole language approaches, and a lot of reading to students in groups. She has parent-teacher conferences coming up and knows that her parents will be eager to find out how their children are doing. She wants to be able to present concrete information to the parents along with her general impressions. So what are the assessment possibilities for this class? Even if you are not a primary school specialist, it might be worthwhile to ponder some of the possibilities. That's what we did. Then we went to the experts and asked some of our friends who are primary teachers to give us some of their ideas. Here are some ideas we came across.

(continued)

One teacher suggested finding reading material that contained a lot of the word attack skills the students were working on or to develop some especially for the class. The teacher could assess progress on the word attack skills in a more natural setting this way. Another teacher suggested keeping track of who goes to the library corner during free time, who can think of a variety of "favorite books," who takes books out of the library on a regular basis, and who appears to be the most engaged in story reading time. A third teacher said she likes to have each student come up for a twenty minute discussion with the teacher where skills can be checked one-on-one during a reading of material constructed for that purpose and an interview about reading interests and practices. A fourth teacher said that she likes to ask which students want to bring in material to read in front of the class. The teacher feels this helps her identify who is feeling good about their reading skills, and allows for some variety in the literacy activity in the class as well.

Setting 2

SAT Math Practice

For our second example, let's stay in the same school district, but move up to the 11th grade and talk about a math class where students are about to take the SATs to improve their chances of getting into college. The instructor has decided that for two weeks prior to the math SAT, 15 minutes of every class period will be dedicated to helping students get ready for the test. He has determined that the best way to get students ready is to have them work on SAT problems that are a little bit beyond their comfort zone. He feels he can stretch their ability by giving them reasonably challenging items to try, then helping them when they run into trouble. Without having studied the scholar, he is effectively incorporating what Vygotsky called the "zone of proximal development" (van der Veer & Valsiner, 1994; Vygotsky, 1978). Just quickly, the zone of proximal development involves the idea of finding what a student can do if assisted by someone more skilled in the task than the student. Thus, with expert help, the student can be successful. We liken this concept to pulling a metal car along with a magnet. You have to keep the magnet just far enough in front of the car to get movement. Too close and the car and the magnet just lock up, too far and the magnet loses its pull. So, for this teacher, the task is to find SAT math items that are at just the right level for students to work on, then have them practice those items with his assistance. Fortunately, this isn't too hard. First, he has to give students a practice version of the SATs and look at the results to find the proper difficulty level for each student. He can also find substantive areas of the test that may be strengths or weaknesses for the student. He can then find sets of other items for students to work on which are just at their level.

This is the first of the assessment tasks, which are appropriate for the learning goals at hand. Then the teacher needs to determine whether the students can work together on solving problems they couldn't solve alone or whether classroom mentors would work in this class. The instructional task at this point becomes finding the best way to help students over the difficulties, which are holding them up on problems (when they encounter problems). The teacher might have to do this alone, or it might be possible for students to help one another. Note that as students are working on problems, they are learning about their own strengths and weaknesses (they are assessing themselves), and when someone is working with them on problems, the mentors (or teacher) are engaging in an immediate assessment activity through their interactions with the students.

Many of the assessments being used in this example are old-fashioned multiple-choice tests, which we would argue are natural assessment in these cases because they stem from the instruction and the instructional needs of the class and because they are consistent with the instructional goals of the class.

We would not want the first-grade teacher to give students multiple-choice reading tests to assess their progress, nor would we want the high school math students to make a video on their favorite calculus problems (OK, some teachers would like to do this, just not us). Natural classroom assessment makes sense in the context of the instruction. It fundamentally cannot be judged outside of that context any more than instruction can be judged outside of the context of the instructional goals it strives to attain (at any rate, we can't think of how it could be). Please note that this does not mean that any assessment given in a classroom is de facto good assessment or good natural assessment. We are not advocates of the "this-is-authentic-assessment-it-doesn't-have-to-be-valid" school of assessment theory. The degree to which we would say that an assessment is good natural assessment is the degree to which it enhances and facilitates the instructional process. To that end, natural assessment often looks a lot like instruction. Frequently, in fact, it *is* instruction—with an assessment lens added to it. This does not have to be the case, but it often is the case.

What Does Assessment Mean for Students? What Can It Mean?

Over our years as educators, we have talked to a lot of students about what assessment means to them. It is not a particularly pretty picture. All too often assessment means an imposition on classroom instruction necessitated by a mandatory grading function. One of our children put it fairly succinctly: "Dad, grading and classroom management are the two things bad teachers can't do." Assessment means a test that has to be studied for, a paper that has to be written, a project that has to be completed. It is work that has to be done. Now in all honesty, none of us is opposed to work, either for us, for our kids, or for other peoples' kids. Work is fine. Not all learning is fun; not all reading is fun (try reading a form from the IRS for fun). However, when the work of learning is done, a student should feel he or she has accomplished something worthwhile, something in keeping with what the class is all about.

"It was hard, but it was fair."

"I didn't always like it, but I'm glad I did it."

"I never studied so hard for a test before."

"I can't believe I actually did that."

These are comments from students we can live with quite happily. Of course, we don't expect to hear them out of second graders too often. At the same time, we have to say we are also quite fond of

"Can we do more of those problems where . . .?"

"Let's try another one of those."

"Did this author write any other stories?"

"Can we write our own stories on this?"

What do we have to do for students to believe that the assessments they are taking are fair? They have to *be* fair. We think this can be accomplished under the following conditions. First, students have to know what the assessment is going to be. If students don't know what the assessment is going to be, they can't really prepare for it. We cannot tell you how many teachers we have encountered who say, "I'm not going to spoonfeed these kids. If I tell them what's going to be on the test, then what am I testing for?" (We often find these same teachers saying, "We tried that here, it didn't work," "I don't teach kids, I teach American history," and "No way the kids in my class could do that." We have colleagues at the university with the same general set of attitudes. We try not to sit next to them at lunch.) What we are saying here is that if students know what they are supposed to be working on and what their teacher thinks is and isn't important, then they will have a better chance to show what they have learned and what they can learn. If you tell them what you think is important to consider in a project, they will work toward the goals you have. If your goal on a particular activity is leaving students to their own invention, then they will give you that. Either way is OK; our point is that what students produce on a project or how they perform on an assessment will be attributable, in part, to the exact nature of the task given to them.

One of the authors of this work has as a learning goal in an experimental psychology class getting all of her students to write in the format of the *Publication Manual of the American Psychological Association (APA)*. This is a complicated style and a very difficult thing to teach to students. She has developed a 45-point checklist of APA style elements. Students are given the checklist and graded using the checklist on each of their seven writing assignments in the class. By the fifth assignment, almost every student is perfect. Now, one could argue that she just told them what she wanted them to do. Or one could argue that by the fifth assignment she isn't getting any differentiation on her scores because almost every one does it almost exactly right. One could argue a lot of things, we suppose. The counterargument is simple. Through a combination of instruction and assessment that were strongly aligned and faithfully executed, a very difficult task was learned by all of the students. They learned how to do this; they can use it in their other psychology and social science classes; and they are proud of themselves for having learned it. Nothing else really matters.

A second aspect to making assessments fair is to make certain they are aligned with the instructional goals and activities of the classroom. Actually, in the eyes of the students, alignment with instruction is more important than alignment with goals. If you have a certain instructional goal and assess it faithfully, but you haven't taught the students how to do it, then the assessment is unfair. On the other hand, if you have a goal and have taught the students something other than that goal, if the assessment matches the instruction, then it is fair. It's not getting you any closer to your goal, but at least it isn't unfair to the students. Assessments should be based clearly on what is going on in the classroom (and outside of it in terms of homework or other learning activities). When students believe assessments are based on what they are being taught and understand the nature of what is expected of them, they believe that the assessment is fair.

How Can Instructional Activities Become Assessment Activities?

This question is actually the topic of the next chapter. We don't want to give away too much in advance, but we want to introduce the idea here that instructional activities and assessment activities need not be too different from one another. In fact, most instructional activities are used by teachers to gather some level of assessment information. When students are working on an activity, most teachers will observe and make assessments about progress as they do. Even when one is engaged in a good old-fashioned lecture to the class, one looks for signs of recognition or confusion on the faces of students. The fundamental idea of *Natural Classroom Assessment* (the book *and* the concept) is that classroom assessment should grow out of classroom instruction.

What Is the Basis for Calling an Assessment Natural?

The basic idea behind natural assessment is the fit between the instruction and the assessment. They should work hand in glove. Often this means that the assessment activity looks a lot like the instructional activity, but this does not necessarily have to be so. We saw some examples earlier in this chapter where the assessment and the instruction were almost indistinguishable, and it is usually the case that this is so. But it could also be the case that the assessment is a type of culminating activity that is different from what has gone on before or is a type of introductory activity that sets the stage for what is to follow. A group-based writing project that is only tangential to a unit on the environment may not be a natural assessment, and a multiple-choice test assessing comprehension of a history unit might be a natural assessment. The essential question that has to be asked of a natural classroom assessment is, "How does this assessment facilitate instruction?" Assessments that exist primarily to put a grade in the grade book or to keep students busy are not natural classroom assessments. Assessments that cause students to work toward accomplishing classroom goals that provide needed information for making instructional decisions that reflect the nature and structure of classroom instruction are natural classroom assessments.

What Is the Role of Motivation in Assessment and Assessment in Motivation?

As we conclude this introductory section and before we move on to the nitty-gritty of the following section, we want to talk a bit about motivation and assessment. This is a difficult topic and one we have spent a fair amount of time investigating (Wolf & Smith, 1995; Wolf, Smith, & Birnbaum, 1995). There is no doubt that assessment causes motivation; it is clear that students are motivated to get the grade, especially at the high school level. The question "Does this count?" is a common one at all grade levels (along with our favorite, "Is this going to be on the test?"). As teachers, we would like our students to be intrinsically motivated, to want to work hard in order to learn, not just to get the grade. But, being practical, we know that this will not always be the case. What we have to think about is the relationship between motivation and assessment. We want assessments that will create motivation by their nature, not ones that motivate simply because they will be counted toward a grade. If you find yourself relying on counting assessments toward grades as a primary means of motivating students to work in the class, it is time to do a thorough reevaluation of what is happening in your classroom. Our guess is that when teachers find themselves in this situation, there are more serious problems than those involving assessment.

What we are striving for in natural classroom assessment is an approach to assessment that creates assessment activities that students regard as naturally motivating. They would be assessments that are fair, challenging, and respectful of students as learners. Students would see them as logically related to the instruction they have been receiving. They would be learning experiences in and of themselves. As teachers, we sometimes have to ask ourselves, "Would I want to be doing this if I were a student in this course?" Sometimes the answer to that question is going to be "no," yet we will still want to use the assessment. That might happen on occasion. But if it does happen, we need to have a strong reason to go ahead and use the assessment. This is where we differ with an assessment approach that is exclusively student centered. As teachers, we need to do things at times that we firmly believe are necessary, but that the students might not agree with. That's OK; it is our responsibility to make such decisions. What we are encouraging teachers to do is to think about every assessment from the students' perspective before implementing it.

CHAPTER 4

Beginning the Design Process

What Are the Characteristics of Good Natural Assessment?

Good natural assessment enhances instruction. It helps children learn. Seems simple enough. But there are several ways in which that might occur. First is the most direct way. The assessment itself can be a good instructional tool. That is, just by engaging in the assessment, the child learns. Thus, an assessment can be a good natural assessment because it looks like instruction. As we have pointed out, it is terrific if it actually is instruction, but has an assessment component to it. (More on this later) This is actually where we started with the idea of natural classroom assessment. We have expanded the notion somewhat, but this is really the heart of the matter: Can you justify this activity as a learning activity? If you can, then it is probably a good natural assessment. At worst, it is probably good instruction. As is always the case with academics, however, we can't leave well enough alone. So we have developed a couple of related ideas.

Think of this first conceptualization of natural assessment as assessment that grows out of an instructional perspective, or is based on instruction. A second way to think about natural assessment is assessment that is complementary to instruction. It is not really the instruction itself, but something that is important to the instructional process. For example, if we are working on a qualitative analysis problem in chemistry (e.g., determining what a mystery substance is), learning how to do a titration is an important part of the process. We may want to have a small assessment on using the equipment for a titration to see if everyone is up to speed on this. It is an integral part of the learning process here, although it is only one of the number of steps in a qualitative analysis.

A third way an assessment can be a natural classroom assessment is if it is an assessment that is a culminating activity. Having worked with students on a variety of the components of an activity, an assessment may involve putting the pieces together in a culminating activity. For example, after working with students on argumentative writing, you may want to give them an assignment to write an op-ed piece for the local newspaper. This may not be exactly what they were working on in their instruction, but you may feel that the transfer is not too great and that a new type of assignment would be beneficial in terms of motivation.

A fourth type of natural classroom assessment is an assessment that tells you where your students are at the beginning of instruction. This can be an introductory activity to a new unit or area of study. You certainly would not count the results toward the grades of students, but it can give you a good idea of where the students are as a group as well as individually. An example of this might be a series of questions requiring estimation, such as the beginning of a mathematics unit on estimation, presented in the form of a game show or an education Olympics.

Now that we have an idea of what some of the assessment activities might be, let's refine the idea of what the characteristics of good natural assessments might look like.

Natural Classroom Assessment

1. Develops naturally from classroom instruction.

2. Respects students.

3. Assesses what students have had the opportunity to learn.

4. Provides students with the opportunity to show what they can do.

5. Facilitates the instructional process.

6. Provides dependable information about students.

Characteristic 1: Natural classroom assessment develops naturally from classroom instruction. Examining this list, we can see from Characteristic 1 that there is typically a strong relationship between instruction and assessment and often a strong resemblance. The logic behind this is as follows. Our instruction should be justifiable from our goals, and so should our assessment be. If this is true, then the two ought to be fairly similar. If they are not, there should be a good reason they are not. (Sometimes there are reasons why they are not. None of these reasons actually comes to mind right now, but we don't want to eliminate the possibility that there might be some.)

Characteristic 2: Natural classroom assessment respects students. We don't like to do things that are boring, unfair, disrespectful, anxiety producing, tedious, or unrelated to our lives, interests, or needs. Sometimes we *have* to do these things, but we don't like them. We especially don't like to go to the

Department of Motor Vehicles, but sometimes we have to. Sometimes assessments are necessary (or mandated) that fit into one of the things-we-don't-want-to-do categories above. If we are going to subject students to such an assessment, we ought to have a really good reason for doing so. It would be much better to have assessments that students considered to be interesting, challenging, worth preparing for, engaging, and relevant to their lives, interests, or needs. This is not a new idea. Some of you may remember John Dewey—we like him. We don't agree with everything he said, but his notion that instruction ought to have some level of authenticity for students seems a quite reasonable proposition to us (1900, 1916, 1938). There are practical as well as philosophical reasons for assessments to be motivating, challenging, and engaging for students Assessments that engage students facilitate the assessment process. If the assessment is not engaging, then we are not sure if we are measuring our goals or if the students were bothering to put in a serious effort (Wolf et al., 1995).

Characteristic 3: Natural classroom assessment assesses what students have had the opportunity to learn. An almost universal complaint heard by students about assessments is that they weren't fair, assessing students on topics they had not learned and not assessing them on topics they had learned. One question to ask yourself is, "Have my students really had a chance to learn this?" There are two caveats to this characteristic. The first is that sometimes we want to do an assessment prior to instruction that provides us with information about where students stand with regard to the material. When we engage in such an assessment, it is only fair to let students know that this is being done and that it will not have negative consequences for them if they do not do well (such as counting for part of their grade). The second caveat is that sometimes we want to assess students' progress as they are working on material to see where we should go next. Again, this should not hold negative consequences for the student. Both of these caveats relate to the notion of formative evaluation, evaluation that is specifically designed to guide instruction, not to make summative judgments about students (see Scriven, 1967).

Characteristic 4: Natural classroom assessment provides students with the opportunity to show what they can do. Fourth, our assessments should provide students with the opportunity to show what they can do. We need to ask ourselves these questions: "What does this assessment require of the students? Does this assessment leave out important learnings from the class? Does everyone have a fair chance to show what they can do?" We would encourage a little empathy when answering. Not sympathy, empathy. Put yourself in your students' shoes. Imagine a student that perhaps does not do his or her best work in one format or another. Is it possible that they know the material, but still might not perform well on the assessment?

Characteristic 5: Natural classroom assessment facilitates the instructional process. We acknowledge that an important part of the instructional process is determining at the end of it how well students have done. It is also critically important to know how well they are doing as they go along. An end-of-unit assessment can encourage students to review material and consolidate their learning, especially if they know what they are supposed to review and consolidate. The question here is, "How will this assessment facilitate the learning of my students?"

Characteristic 6: Natural classroom assessment provides dependable information about students. Finally, we ask whether the assessment is providing the information that we need and providing it in a dependable fashion. This is where we look at some of the more traditional issues in assessment but perhaps in a new light.* There are a couple of components to this issue. First, let's ask if the assessment is really measuring what we have been teaching students. In traditional assessment language, this is a question of validity. There are a lot of ways to look at validity, but we are going to look at it strictly from an instructional perspective. Basically, there are two questions you can pose of an assessment from an instructional validity perspective. The first one is, "Does this assessment measure what I want the students to be learning?" Does it cover the learning, all of the learning, and only the learning? If it does, then you should be in pretty good shape. A second, related question that can be posed is, "Does this assessment cause my students to engage in the learning activities I want them to be engaged in?" How are these questions different? The first question (Does this cover all the learning and only the learning?) concerns the issue of an assessment that accurately reflects what the instruction is. Although the assessment used may be quite imaginative, the purpose of the assessment is to check to see if the material has been mastered. The second question (Does this assessment cause my students to engage in appropriate learning activities?) imagines an assessment that is part of the learning process itself, one that may even break new ground for the students. What we are saying here is that it is OK for the assessment to actually be instruction in an area. Important concept—let's highlight it.

> Assessment is part of instruction.

You might be tempted to say, "How can assessment *not* be part of instruction?" If you have such a temptation, you are in synch with what we are trying to say. You also might be tempted to say, "Didn't you say the exact same thing a couple of chapters ago?" We did. We like reinforcement.

There are other components of good natural classroom assessments in Characteristic 6, "The Really Long Characteristic." One is that good natural classroom assessments provide enough information about the students. Some examples might help here. If you say, "Does everybody get that? OK, good, let's move on," some students may be reluctant to indicate that they

---

* This is a really long characteristic. In fact, people have written whole books about this topic. We're just warning you now in case you get lost in a couple of pages.

didn't get it. Another example might be a short quiz at the end of a long and complex unit. The quiz itself may useful, but maybe it just wasn't long enough to really tap into what was going on in the unit. Here the question is, "Do I have enough information on the students in regard to this learning?" Related to this concern is a concern about format. We encourage you to mix up your formats for assessing students. Just as some students don't really do their best on a multiple-choice test, other students don't do their best in a journal, or in work done with other students. It can be a real revelation to see a student's work come to life when assessed in a fashion that fits well with the student.

The final concern on validity is fairness to all students. This is the issue related to bias. As teachers, we like to think that we are sensitive to issues of bias. We work hard to make sure that students whose color, ethnicity, gender, or abilities are different from ours get the same opportunity to do well in our class. As teachers, we are pretty good at stopping and thinking about such things. We need to make sure that we think about them in terms of assessment as well. We need to put ourselves in the shoes of our students and walk through our assessments. Furthermore, we would encourage you to consider some new groups of students as well: students who are shy, who don't write well, who don't like to speak in front of the class, who have difficulty finding time for homework or projects to be completed at home, who don't own a home computer, who are not creative, who don't have parents who insist that homework get done, who don't have parents who help them with the assessment project to be completed at home, who can't get onto the Internet. This may seem like an imposing list, and for some aspects of it, a teacher might reasonably say, "But my students have to do homework in order to learn." This is true and you might want to use the advantages of the Internet for those students who have it. We cannot focus all instruction on the most needy student. But—*and this is an important "but"*—when it comes time to assess students on what they can do, we need to be especially careful that we afford all students an equal opportunity to show what they can do. If the sixth-grade science fair projects are 60% parent and 40% student, is it fair to draw conclusions about student ability from this? If students have to give a presentation on their social studies project, is it fair to say that a student did not learn the material when the fact of the matter is that she is upset over being teased because she is overweight and doesn't want to stand up in front of the class? If one student has a computer with a grammar and spelling checker, and another does not have a computer at all, how can we make fair assessments about these two students on a writing assignment done at home, especially one that requires several revisions?

The purpose here is not to handcuff teachers into not being able to do anything. The purpose here is to encourage a review of any assessment activity to see how vulnerable it is to this kind of problem, then to work to minimize the effects of the problem. There are usually ways to work around the problems that might be encountered. First, check to see if there are problems. In many school districts, all or almost all of the students will have a computer and Internet access. If not, sometimes arrangements can be made. Students who feel they are not good at presenting in front of the class can perhaps be assessed through a different format (although you may still want to encourage a presentation to build up confidence; just don't do the assessment on it). Most problems can be addressed with a little creative problem solving. One caution before leaving this topic: Homework and projects done at home can be a great source of invalidity in assessments. We strongly recommend communicating to parents about how you want them to help on a project or on homework. As parents, we were never quite sure what various teachers wanted us to do in terms of helping (or not helping) our own children.

We warned you that this would be a bit long, but it is our only major exploration of technical issues associated with assessment. Let's summarize. By saying we want to be sure that assessments are providing us with what we want, we are basically saying that we want assessments

1. That cover what we are teaching, only what we are teaching, and all of what we are teaching (validity)

2. That provide us with sufficient information to make good instructional decisions (reliability)

3. That provide all children with as equal an opportunity as possible to show us what they can do (freedom from bias)

There, that wasn't too bad.

Where Do We Start When Developing Assessments?

If there is one idea we wish to communicate in this small book, it is that good assessments should begin with instructional goals and instruction. Most teachers we have talked to believe in their ability to teach, but are a little leery about their ability to develop good assessments. Many of them have never had any course work on assessment. Our purpose here is to say

> Play from your strength.

Play from your strength is actually a bridge term (the card game, not the spans across water) that means to play the suit that is powerful in your hand. For our purposes, it means to start thinking about assessment by thinking about instruction and instructional goals. Let's look at a few examples of what this might mean.

Getting Started on Assessments: Example 1

Perspective Taking in The Scarlet Letter

We're reading *The Scarlet Letter* in our eighth-grade literacy skills class, and one of the aspects we are focused on is the sense of the townspeople in their reactions to Hester Prynne. From a modern sensibility, the townspeople seem to be narrow-minded, unforgiving, and somewhat nasty. It may be hard for students to understand how a group of people could hold these attitudes. One of our instructional goals concerns developing in students the ability to take perspectives other than their own, and this seems like an excellent opportunity. From an instructional perspective, what we have been doing in class is talking about the feelings of the townspeople: Why are they so opposed to Hester Prynne and her child? What is it about their lives, their society, even their religious beliefs that makes them so hostile? It is not hard to take Hester's perspective since she is a sympathetic character, but what about the characters who are less sympathetic? That has been our instructional goal and some of the instructional activity for Example 1.

Getting Started on Assessments: Example 2

Other Places, Other People

For a second example, let's look at a fifth-grade social studies class. Our instructional goal here is getting our students out of their town, state, and even country to look at the world. We want them to get an idea of what it would be like to live in a different country. More formally, our instructional goal is for students to comprehend the social, economic, and political differences between the United States and other countries. We have been looking at five ways in which the lives of people who live in other countries are different from ours. Our focus has been on diet, currency, social customs, occupations, and the role of children. From an instructional perspective, we have taken one country, Mexico, and looked at all of these issues as a class. We used the Internet, the local library, and two classmates who have relatives living in Mexico as resources. Then the class was broken down into four research teams to look at four more countries. Their task was to replicate the process of the Mexico work and make a report to the class as a whole.

Getting Started on Assessments: Example 3

Preparation for Math SAT

For our third example, we choose preparation for the math SAT for our high school junior year Algebra II class. This is a college prep class, but not an accelerated or honors class. We choose this in part because it represents a very applied challenge and in part because it allows for thinking outside of the box on assessment. Our instructional goal is straightforward and very much on the minds of the students: improving SAT math scores for students who are about to take the SATs. Our instruction has stayed fairly close to the instructional goal. We have been practicing a variety of SAT math items by having the students work on a small set, then reviewing the work during class time.

That should provide us with enough material to work on. Let's see what the next issue is.

What Are the Options That Are Available?

There are a lot of options available. We present a dozen here and are probably still missing a few. Let's take a quick look at these possibilities:

1. **Essays** allow you to see how students develop ideas around a theme and how well they can present those ideas in written form. A well-constructed essay assessment can provide insight into the nature and structure of student ideas and knowledge on a given topic. Be careful not to confound writing ability with knowledge and skills in the subject area. Also, be sure that the essay topic really engages the student and is clearly focused so that you get what you want.

2. **Journals** allow for tracking student responses to instruction on an ongoing basis. They can provide insight into the problems students are having and how they are reacting to those problems as well as documenting student growth. Be careful that journals do not become burdensome to students (especially those who do not like to write) and that they are not used for amateur psychology.

3. **Multiple-choice** tests can allow you to assess breadth of knowledge in a subject area in a relatively quick and objective fashion. Well-constructed multiple-choice tests can provide information on whether students grasp the content of a unit. Be careful that questions are phrased clearly and that the

right answer is clearly right. Also, be careful not to use tests that come with instructional materials unless you have reviewed the materials carefully.

4. **Performances** are a great way to change the usual instructional and assessment practice and allow students to express creativity. They can provide you with insights into student abilities that might not be tapped in any other way. Be careful not to confuse content mastery with expressive or creative ability. Also be careful to make sure that the performance really relates to instructional goals and is not simply entertainment. (Some entertainment is fine in class, but it usually doesn't contribute much to assessment issues.) By the way, by *performances* here we mean real performances, not performance assessment. Many of these 12 ideas are forms of performance assessment, and we cover that in the next chapter.

5. **Projects** are one of our favorite forms of assessment. In addition to content mastery, it provides the opportunity to see how well organized the student is. Can he or she "put it all together" to get the project done? This is a frequently overlooked aspect of instruction. For college students (and in life), this ability is critical, yet it is often overlooked in instruction and assessment. Be certain to explain what you want and how the project is going to be graded. Also be careful that the work is actually the work of the student. If you are going to permit outside help, be explicit about what is and isn't allowed. Keep in mind that younger students may lack the planning skills necessary to execute a long-term project without substantial assistance from you.

6. **True-or-false tests,** on the other hand, are one of our least favorite forms of assessment. About the only good thing we can think of to say about true-or-false tests is that you can ask a lot of questions in a short amount of time. Be sure the true statements are really true and the false ones, false. Also be careful that your students don't leave the assessment "believing" in their incorrect answers.

7. **Short-answer tests** are the real workhorse of teacher-made assessments. In professional literature, these are now called *constructed response* items because the student has to—you guessed it—construct a response. Advantages are that students have to come up with the right answer (as opposed to identifying it in a multiple-choice list) and that the format gives you a lot of flexibility. Be careful to be specific in what you are looking for in the right answer, or you may find yourself having to give partial or full credit for answers that you didn't really want but that are technically correct responses. For example, if you ask "What is William Henry Harrison known for?" you could get all sorts of answers, even though the answer you want is "Hero of Tippecanoe."

8. **Group work** allows for the strengths of several people to be brought to a problem or task and helps to develop the ability to work in groups, an essential life skill. Group projects can engender real pride in accomplishments of

the group and can be great for self-esteem, especially for group members who face special challenges. Be careful that you are not just getting the efforts of one or two people in the group and in how you assign grades to the group as a whole.

9. **Posters** can be used to allow students the ability to present what they know about a topic in a "mixed-media" format and allows others to see their work. Poster fairs are a nice way to celebrate and communicate what everyone has been working on in class. Be careful to be clear about how you are going to grade the posters, what materials should (or should not) be used, and how much outside help is permissible in the development of the posters.

10. **Reaction papers** might be thought of as a type of limited journal entry. They call for a student to say what he or she thinks about a topic, an event, or an issue that has come out in class. They provide the opportunity to use analytical skills and persuasive writing. Be careful that students understand what they are to do and how they will be graded, and that they have had instruction on what good and bad papers look like.

11. **Labs** are typically considered to be the domain of the sciences, but the ideas of a lab can be extended to a variety of subject areas. Labs are an excellent blend of instruction and assessment. Be careful not to just have students be completing a "recipe" of tasks and seeing what happens. Labs should have a purpose related to instructional goals and should work toward the development of those goals.

12. **Reports** are another workhorse of classroom assessment. Like projects, reports require students to learn about a topic, to develop their thoughts about the topic, and to put those thoughts in writing in a clear fashion. Often students have to support their ideas with reference work. Reports provide the opportunity to see if students can learn on their own and if they can communicate clearly. Organizational and writing skills are at a premium, as is follow-through. Be careful not to confuse good writing ability with what may be a superficial knowledge of the topic or vice versa.

How Do the Options Relate to Different Goals?

Now that we have seen what the options are, how do we select the ones we want to use in any particular situation? Well, we can't cover all possible situations, but let's look at the three examples given earlier and see how the options relate to those goals.

We start with Example 1, *The Scarlet Letter.* We were working on the ability to take the perspective of others, and *The Scarlet Letter* afforded an opportunity to do this with a group of others that weren't particularly sympathetic, the townspeople. In our instruction, we might have been talking about the need for people in a small community to abide by the rules of the community, just as we have rules for the community of the class. We might also have talked about how students themselves might not be behaving in a kind fashion toward someone from outside their circle of friends. Or we might have talked about how people might be threatened by those who break the rules of a religion.

The question now comes up as to how we are going to assess this aspect of instruction. How can we determine the extent to which students have learned how to take the perspective of another? There are a number of possibilities here. Consider for a moment the following options and how you might implement them: essay, journal, performance, project, lab. For an essay, you might take a particular minor character in the book and ask that the student write a diary entry about what is going on in town as that character. For journal entries, you might ask students at several points in the instructional process to write how they feel about the townspeople and their perspective on the issue. You can look for growth in the ability to take the perspective of the townspeople. For a performance, you could have a group of students develop a skit where a child in the family of one of the townspeople asks at the dinner table why someone has been mean to Hester Prynne in town. A mother, a father, an older sibling, and a neighbor might be present at the dinner table. For a project, you might assign students the task of finding an international conflict or issue and to take the side of one group or another and present their argument on the issue. These projects can then be brought together or presented to see how various sides of an issue can all seem reasonable. For a lab, you can use software such as SimCity, which requires the player(s) to build a town with limited resources. Each decision that is made has consequences for the player. For example, you can build a school or a library, but both will cost tax dollars, which may result in increased taxes. This leads to voter discontent. Competing interests must be balanced. The players are required to take the perspective of all concerned in making decisions.

Each of these options has strengths and weaknesses, but we can see that each relates to the goal of seeing how well students are getting the idea of taking the perspective of others. For this objective, a multiple-choice or short-answer test may not get at the depth of the issue nearly as well as some of the other options.

In Example 2, we were interested in getting students to look at how other people live. Here our objectives are related to understanding how other people live and developing the ability to learn about other countries (what are the resources available and how do we access them). In this example, an assessment using a poster format might be ideal. Each student can be assigned a country or choose from a list of countries (open choice might result in some students picking particularly difficult or easy countries). They can be assigned the task of learning about the country and developing a poster that presented their information in an appealing fashion. They might also be asked to make a short presentation about the country. Group work has already been used instructionally in this example, but it is another good possibility for assessment. Groups can be constructed anew and new countries can be given to each group. The groups can make presentations on their countries. Students can be required to take notes on the countries presented, and a multiple-choice test might follow. If the primary goal is learning that other countries are different from us, then the multiple-choice test might be of less value. If learning some specifics about the other countries is important (and in all honesty, we would argue that it is), then a multiple-choice or short-answer test would be a good way to assess knowledge of the countries.

In Example 3 we were interested in developing SAT math test ability. Obviously, multiple-choice SAT items are going to be an essential ingredient in any assessment of this instruction, but there are some other possibilities as well. What is the instructional goal? To get students to perform better on these items. Different students are going to have different types of difficulties here (Gallagher & De Lisi, 1994). It might be useful to have students keep a journal of the kinds of problems they feel they are having. You can use the journal to help guide instruction. Group work and performances might be useful here as well. A contest could be held to see how many really tough items could be solved in 15 minutes by teams of students. The idea is to get students to work together to share their abilities. Performance is another possibility. The best way to see what students' difficulties are is to watch students try to solve problems. For example, have a student explain his or her efforts at the board. Then you, and the other students as well, can see the thought processes underlying the work. When the student knows how to solve the problem, others can learn from his or her success. When the student runs into difficulty, you can pinpoint that difficulty and help him or her through it. Chances are that others in the class were having the same difficulty. Another very helpful outcome here is that sometimes students have better heuristics for solving these problems than we do. When they explain how they do their work at the board, or when another student offers help, these effective problem-solving approaches become public.

Back in Chapter 1, we talked about the fact that sometimes teachers don't develop their own objectives; they work with ones given to them by the school, the district, and increasingly, the state. Before we leave this chapter, we want to walk through several examples showing how natural classroom assessment might be based on state standards as opposed to standards developed by the teachers. In our two examples, the teachers, the schools, and the towns are made up, but the states and the state standards are real. (Actually, we do use the names of two teachers we like a lot.)

Setting One

Mrs. DeCosta's Fourth Grade Class at Stanton
Elementary School in Martindale, Vermont

Mrs. DeCosta teaches fourth grade in Martindale, Vermont, an imaginary small town of roughly 25,000 people in southern Vermont. She uses the Vermont State Standards (Vermont State Department of Education, 1999) as goals for her teaching and is in the process of looking at an idea she has for teaching in the area of social studies and reasoning and problem solving. The library board of Martindale has proposed a $2.4 million bond issue to build an expansion onto the library to increase space for books and to add a technology center. A group of citizens in town opposes the bond issue because it will be too heavy a tax burden, particularly for the elderly, and because the construction of the expansion will result in the loss of part of a small park that adjoins the library. Mrs. DeCosta thinks this setting provides an excellent opportunity for her students to work on the development of the following state standards in the areas of history and social sciences and reasoning and problem solving.

History and Social Science Standards

6.1   Students examine complex webs of causes and effects in relation to events to generalize about the workings of human societies, and they apply their findings to problems.

6.2   Students understand the varied uses of evidence and data and use both to make interpretations concerning public issues.

6.3   Students analyze knowledge as a collection of selected facts and interpretations based on a particular historical or social setting.

6.10 Students examine and debate the meaning of citizenship and act as citizens in a democratic society.

6.11 Students analyze the access that various groups and individuals have had to justice, reward, and power, as those are evident in the institutions in various times in their local community, in Vermont, in the United States, and in various locations worldwide.

6.20 Students analyze the nature of conflicts, how they have been or might be resolved, and how some have shaped the divisions in various times of their local community, Vermont, the United States, and the world.

Reasoning and Problem-Solving Standards

2.1 Students ask a variety of questions.

2.2 Students use reasoning strategies, knowledge, and common sense to solve complex problems related to all fields of knowledge.

2.3 Students devise and test ways of improving the effectiveness of a system (Vermont State Department of Education, 1999).

It may be the case that there are other standards being worked toward here, but nine ought to get us started. Mrs. DeCosta believes that having her students examine the issues related to the library expansion bond issue will allow them to work on skills related to the standards above in a fashion that will be engaging and of personal relevance to them. At the same time that she wants them working on a real-life topic, she acknowledges that the library issue is a means to an end. Her responsibility as a teacher is not to impact the library bond issue, but to develop the skills in her students that will enable them to look not only at this issue but also at others as they grow up. Therefore, she is concerned not just with getting them engaged in this activity, but with making certain that skills develop out of these activities.

Mrs. DeCosta decides that this activity might be a good example of using problem-based learning. She divides the class into four teams:

1. A pro-expansion team

2. An anti-expansion team

3. A team of reporters writing about the issue

4. A team of technical experts on libraries and technology

She has 20 students in the class, so each team will have five members. Each team has to begin by generating, with Mrs. DeCosta, what they see as their essential task or problem to solve, then determining what resources exist to bring to bear on the problem, how they are going to divide their tasks and assign responsibilities, and what organizational structure and time frame they will work under. They will then move on to doing the work they have devised. And Mrs. DeCosta wants the students to think about what they are doing as they do it, so each student has two additional components to his or her work. First, each student must contribute to an online discussion on the issue on the classroom Web site. They can make their contributions during the school day, or in the evening by using their home computer, or the two that are currently in the town library. In this discussion, they will step out of their roles as team members and talk about the issue from their own perspective. Second, each student will keep a notebook on his or her progress on the team activity.

Setting Two

Mr. Linton's Sixth-Grade Language Arts in Rawlings, Ohio

Mr. Linton teaches in the imaginary Cincinnati suburb of Rawlings, Ohio. Mr. Linton uses the Sixth-Grade Learning Outcomes objectives from the State of Ohio Department of Education (1999) as his learning goals in the area of writing. Based on the work that his students had turned in the first couple months of the 1999–2000 school year, he believes that most of his students have the basics down as far as their reaching his goals for them, but that their writing could be sharper, cleaner, speak with a clearer sense of audience, and generally be more interesting to read. At the same time, a few of the students still need some work on the basics, and all of the students could experiment a bit more with a broader variety of sentence types. He wants to engage his students in writing tasks that they would find interesting and useful while showing them how they can improve their work with a little more thought and effort. Looking at the state standards, he finds that he will be working on the following:

> The student will use the writing process to make the writing activities clear for the intended audience, as evidenced by the capacity to
>
> a. Focus on the topic with adequate supporting ideas or examples
>
> b. Exhibit a logical organizational pattern that demonstrates a sense of flow and conveys a sense of completeness and wholeness
>
> c. Exhibit word choice appropriate to the subject, the purpose, and the intended audience
>
> d. Communicate clarity of thought
>
> e. Use complete sentences except where purposeful phrases or clauses are desirable

h. Include sentences of varied length and structure (Ohio State Department of Education, 1999)

(Objectives f and g relate to handwriting and spelling, topics Mr. Linton is not as concerned with for this assignment.)

At the same time that he wants to work on his goals for his students in writing, Mr. Linton also is working on some of the goals in the area of citizenship. He'd like his students to focus their efforts on one or more of these goals and finds the following might be quite suitable:

Identify a significant individual from a region of the world other than North America and discuss cause-and-effect relationships surrounding a major event in the individual's life (Ohio State Department of Education, 1999).

Mr. Linton has decided to combine these objectives into a classroom activity. Each student has to pick a person from a region of the world other than North America and write a summary of the person's life, focusing on a major event in that person's life. The student will select his or her individual with Mr. Linton's help to ensure that there is enough information available to be able to do a good job. When everyone is done, they will put the pieces together to make a class book, something like "Looking Abroad: Critical Events in the Lives of Famous People." Mr. Linton feels that if his students would focus more on what they need to do to make their writing better, they would see improvement in their work. He decides to make writing/editing teams out of the class. Each team will have four members and will work on these aspects:

1. Does the basic piece contain the appropriate aspects of the assignment?
2. Is there a logical flow to the presentation of the material?
3. Could there be more supporting details?
4. Could sentence length be more varied, and could more interesting words be used?

Mr. Linton feels that if everyone works on one aspect of another team member's paper, then each student will grow with respect to the instructional goals, and each student's paper and, more important, writing skills will benefit from the feedback. Another option is to work more analytically on skills. This could be done by giving students simple sentences and asking them to elaborate on them or to improve the vocabulary. Another approach might be to provide students with papers and ask them to grade the papers according to the instructional goals listed above. Students could also be asked to assess their own work with respect to the goals and to determine for themselves the areas they feel they could improve.

Our goal in this chapter was to reinforce a tighter fit between assessment and instruction by showing how assessment should start with instruction and instructional goals. We also looked at the characteristics we want in a good natural classroom assessment and how state standards could lead to natural classroom assessment. Whenever we have a question about an assessment activity, we should return to the instructional goal and make sure that we are getting what we want. The key here is to play from strength; if you know how to teach, basically you also know how to assess.

CHAPTER 5

Choosing Performance/ Authentic Assessments/ Projects

In this chapter, we are going to look at performance/authentic assessments and/or projects. We don't usually write sentences with two slashes as we did in the sentence above, but there is a bit of a nomenclature problem here that needs to be resolved before we can go much further. The problem is what to call those assessments that sometimes get called performance assessment, sometimes alternative assessment, occasionally authentic assessment, and that often simply seem to be those things we used to call "projects." Well, to begin, names don't bother us a whole lot; in fact, we invented the term "natural assessment" for this book. There has been something of an orthodoxy conflict in the field of assessment over this issue and we want to stake out our position on this unambiguously: we don't care much. When the minirevolution in assessment began, alternative assessment was very popular. Now that this form of assessment has become fairly widely used, it doesn't seem so alternative anymore. Authentic assessment seemed to strike a nice contrast with assessment that wasn't authentic, but folks were not quite sure as to what one was being authentic to, so at the time of this writing, performance assessment seems to be winning out—but stay tuned. And finally, portfolio assessment is a popular idea as well. It stands somewhat apart from this nomenclature fray, as it is fairly specifically defined. *Portfolios* are a collection of information that present students' range of accomplishments and activities. (The only term you might confuse it with is *folder*. Folder? Yep, folder. That's what a portfolio was called when we were in school. It was where you kept your work. But whatever you call them, we like them, as they allow a child, a parent, or a teacher the opportunity to look at where the child was coming from and where he or she is today.)

In this chapter, we are going to look at what we will call performance assessment and not worry about whether we have the term that is currently most popular. You are not necessarily observing a performance in performance assessment, although you might be. The idea behind performance assessment is that the students have actually done whatever it is that you want them to be able to do, as opposed to an approximation. This is not to say that some performance assessments are not without their own levels of artificiality, but the idea is to keep the assessment as close as possible to the skills, knowledge, and abilities that are of interest. It usually involves either the demonstration of these skills, knowledge, and abilities in a directly observable fashion or the completion of some product that can then be evaluated.

Are Performance Assessments the Most Natural Form of Assessment?

Probably.

We'd love to leave this section with just that one word answer, but if we did they might throw us out of the college professors' club (and it took so long to learn the secret handshake). You may have been noticing that we have two kinds of assessment evolving out of our concept of natural classroom assessment. The first kind of assessment either mimics or is actually part of the instructional process. The second kind of assessment is used to directly affect the instructional process and may or may not look like the instruction itself. The first kind is most likely to be what people call performance assessment, in that it would typically involve directly observable demonstrations of competence. The second is natural as well in that it is a natural part of the instructional process. It is important to point out that you could have a performance assessment that was only marginally related to what you were trying to accomplish in the classroom. In this case, it wouldn't be natural; in fact, it would be bogus. We are arguing here that the more an assessment can be justified based on its instructional value, the more it can be considered a natural assessment. A logical extension of this idea is that assessment that is combined with ongoing instruction may be the most natural form of assessment.

The concept of performance assessment has been around for a little more than a decade at the time of this writing, and many classroom teachers have been catching onto a secret about it.

> You've been doing it for years.

True enough. It's the field of education as taught in schools of education that has just recently caught up. *If you really want to see where performance assessment has been turned into an art form, go to an art class.* Art teachers teach kids about art and how to do art. (Actually, there are some interesting battles within art education over what is proper instruction, but that's another book.) They teach techniques and watch students practice the techniques, making constructive criticism as they go. Students are given assignments to complete, and then the completed project is evaluated by the teacher, sometimes solely for purposes of improving the students' technique (formative assessment) and other times for purposes of a grade (summative assessment). The assignments that the students turn in *are in and of themselves* reflective of the instructional goals of the class. Sometimes students undertake exercises such as drawing a hand or a crumpled piece of paper. These are component pieces of the overall goals (although we have seen many studies of isolated body parts in the world's famous museums). Sometimes students will draw or paint an entire human figure, other times they will be free to compose their own works as well as be responsible for their execution. These are essays in much the same sense that a written exposition is. And finally, work is accumulated in a portfolio, sometimes just as a working record and storage place, other times as a portfolio for show or evaluation. When it comes to being progressive and innovative in the field of classroom assessment, the art teacher has been doing it for years. If you don't get along with the art teacher, try the music teacher, the shop teacher, the band director, or one of the coaches. They live by the concept of performance assessment.

The perceptive reader may be asking, "Have I really been doing all this good stuff in my classroom?" Stop and think about it for a second. What *do* you do in your classroom in terms of assessment? Go ahead, think about it. This is one of those times in the book where we would like you to be a little bit contemplative. Make a list of five different assessment activities you have engaged in recently. Now ask some questions about your list. How much variety in format do you have? How many of these assessments also serve as good instructional practice? How many got the students excited about what they were doing? How many really gave you solid information about how well the students were doing? How many of them fit really well with the instructional process? How many facilitated instruction? How many allowed students to really show what they could do? Who knows, maybe you can put this book down right now. But maybe there are one or two or even more times when you might be saying, "I probably could have done that one better." That's OK. Nobody's perfect. If this were easy, politicians could do it. Besides, really good assessment takes time, effort, and creativity. Baby steps. A little bit at a time.

How Can I Juggle the Competing Demands of Fidelity to Instruction, the Need for Information, and the Simple Requirements of Time and Effort?

This isn't easy. We have a couple of ideas here, though. First, accumulate. You can accumulate in three ways we can think of right off. Getting older is one way. Whenever you have a good assessment idea, be sure to save it for following years and look for ways to expand on it. If you are a preservice teacher reading this book, you might be saying, "Oh, great, I'll have this down by the time I'm 40 and then I'll be too old to remember anything." Every member of your humble author team is over 40 and none of us has forgotten anything we can think of. A second way to accumulate is to borrow from colleagues. One of the truly great things about the field of education is that almost everyone in it is willing to share. OK, maybe not old Mrs. Whizzler, but pretty much everybody else. Go ask. A third way to accumulate is through the vast array of teacher resources available through teacher networks and now through the Internet. You simply do not have to invent all of this stuff yourself. Get help.

The second way to address this problem is by letting instruction be assessment. We've been harping on this for a good 30 pages or so by now, so it's probably getting through—maybe even becoming tedious. But, as you know by now, when you are developing your instructional activities, you should always take time to put on your assessment glasses to look at what's going on. We have provided a number of examples in previous chapters, but it can't hurt to consider a couple more. We'll do that in the next section.

A third way to address the problem of juggling competing demands is to *do less, better.* This is kind of radical, so you may want to keep it under your hat. The superficial coverage of a wide variety of objectives is usually not as helpful to students as thorough coverage of fewer objectives. Now, you might not have a lot of control over the number of goals you are supposed to cover, but if you do, take the time to think about, "What if I dropped these two goals and concentrated my efforts on doing a terrific job on these four?" Related to this idea is the need to make sure that students understand the possible extensions, ramifications, similarity to other situations, and general potential for transfer that exists in what they are currently learning. If you want students to be able to carry over their learning from one area to another, *teach them how to do it.* If they already knew how to do it, they wouldn't be kids, they would be short adults. We could continue on this topic, but we have to get to other things.

How Can Strong Performance Assessments Be Constructed?

First off, it is hard to tell if a performance assessment is good unless you know about the instruction to which it is related. This is actually true of all assessment, but it seems particularly true of performance assessment, which has as one of its hallmarks its faithfulness to instruction. We are going to recommend that you begin the construction of performance assessments by thinking really hard about these two questions:

1. What do I want students to be able to do?

2. What have we been doing instructionally to learn this material?

The first question concerns the relationship between the assessment and the goal. It looks at the content of the assessment. It gets at what you want students doing in the assessment. This is an invaluable touchstone in determining whether you are really getting what you want in an assessment. Look at what students will be doing and what you will be assessing them on and ask yourself these additional questions: "Is this really what I want students to be able to do? If a student can do well on this task, has he or she really achieved the goal that was set? If a student does not do well on this task, do I really know that he or she hasn't achieved the goal?"

The second question, "What have we been doing instructionally to learn this material?" looks at the relationship between the assessment and the instruction that has been occurring in the classroom. It concerns the form or structure of the assessment. The further the assessment departs from the nature of the classroom instruction, the more likely extraneous variables are entering into the equation. That is, some students who know the material may not do well on the form of the assessment and others may seem to know the material because they are particularly good at the format.

One of the major problems in the research literature on performance assessment is that one performance assessment in a given area, say science, does not relate very strongly to another performance assessment in the same area. That is, if a group of students are given two performance assessments in the same area, the correlation between their performances on these two assessments is not very high (Shavelson, Baxter, & Pine, 1991). Although this has become a major concern for people who do measurement for a living, we are less concerned because these performance assessments typically have been created independent of a specific course of learning. They are more or less generic performance assessments to see how well students are doing in a subject matter generally. Since we don't think you can judge the quality of a performance assessment without knowing what went on instructionally with the students, the lack of correlation is what we would expect. If you are trying out a generic assessment with students from different schools, it might well be the case that some students will have more of the skills and knowledge for assessment A than assessment B, and other students, the reverse.

We are concerned with assessing students on those things that we know we have taught them. If our instruction has been true to our instructional goals and if the assessment is true to the instructional goals and to the nature of instruction, it should be useful as an assessment tool in our classroom.

So you've done that—what's next? Next is constructing a task for students that allows them to demonstrate that they have achieved the instructional goal, or at any rate, the part of current interest. An example might be helpful.

Let's say that we have been teaching research and library skills to our sopho-more American history students. We would like to see if they can put these skills to use, since our instructional goal says that students should be able to use the library and other resources to research a topic. So what do we do? Well, we probably want to construct a task that requires them to do this. There are a number of options here. We could assign a research paper on a common topic assigned to the whole class. What are the pros and cons of this approach? To begin, it would certainly require students to obtain the necessary informa-tion. That's good. But, students might just pool their efforts and let the one or two kids who are really good at this do all the work. That's bad. Not that group-based work is bad, but this clearly would not be what we want. If everyone has the same task, we know that the amount of information available and the ease of obtaining it would be the same for everyone (if they worked independently) and that would be good. But the potential for some students to simply borrow someone else's work is probably too great a problem. We probably need to make a revision here. What about each student writing a research paper on this topic? Well, we are all for a lot of writing, but there is a potential confound here. What about students who are excellent writers, but don't really know how to get the research? What about students who are excellent researchers, but can't write? Another problem, perhaps. What if the topic is boring, or bor-ing to some students and exciting to others?

Let's revise the assignment. First, what are we going to do about the writ-ing problem? A possibility is breaking the assignment into two parts, a research component and a writing component. You might note that many newspapers and news magazines note at the end of an article that some people contrib-uted to the research on the article, while others wrote. There is a role out there for both skills, although both in one person is ideal. The next issue is having everyone do the same topic. On one hand, it's fair to everyone because the same information is available to all; on the other hand, it's not fair because some students will borrow from others and, also, the topic may be boring for some. And we might be taxing the resources of the school and town libraries. Let's think about moving to a list of topics and having each student pick a dif-ferent topic, or even suggesting their own. They can be assigned to conduct a preliminary investigation phase to look for information. If it looks good, they can continue; if it looks like there won't be enough information, they can move to a more tried and true topic (this is where having accumulated information on what will work and what won't is helpful).

Let's look at a second example. Let's move from research and writing skills in a 10th-grade American history class to word problems in 6th-grade math class. On the face of it, this might seem quite straightforward. If you've been doing word problems in instruction, it would be useful to do some for assess-ment as well. Fair enough, but let's see if we can look a little deeper into this. What is the instructional goal here? "The student can do word problems in math" might be OK for starters, but is that really what we are after? In all honesty, there are no math word problems in real life. There aren't even all that many after high school. Maybe we're after the ability to analyze problems to see what is being asked, to restructure information to make it more useful, to develop a plan of attack for a problem, to be able to estimate reasonable answers, to evaluate our work against our estimates, to be comfortable working in the quantitative domain where answers tend to actually be right or wrong. Maybe we're not after those things at all, but if you think about it, those are skills that are useful in later schooling and in life. We hope that they are the actual goals in some states, districts, schools, or, at best, in the minds of teachers.

If the instructional goal is just to do word problems and if the nature and structure of those problems is fairly well specified (and often this is the case), then you can just get on with it. It shouldn't be hard to develop the assessment here, although you do want to make sure that the vocabulary or reading comprehension necessary to solve the problem isn't too demanding. But if some of those other ideas are more what you are after, then you might have a different task facing you, instructionally as well as in terms of assessment. To get after some of these instructional goals, you might want to vary the nature of the problems. You might want to have students just estimate answers to some problems. You might want to provide the work and thinking of an imaginary student who has made a mistake and have your student find the flaw in the thinking. As your instructional goal becomes more interesting, more challenging, and more useful to students, so does your assessment.

To recap, what do you really want students to be able to do, and how have you been teaching it? These two concepts guide the development of the performance assessment.

Where Do I Go Next in the Process?

The next step is to structure the task. What exactly are you going to require of students? What are you going to give them to set up the task? What resources are available to them? What is it that you expect in the way of a product? What are you going to value in their response and what is not important and less important? If you tell students what you want you are more likely to get it than if you make them guess. Ask yourself this question, "Is one of my instructional goals that students should be able to divine what I think is important and what is not?" In inservice workshops when we go over this some faculty say, "I'm not going to spoon-feed this to these people. They'll never learn anything on their own." Heavens to Betsy—we don't want any spoon-feeding! What we want are clear directions, clear expectations, fairness, no tricks—in a phrase, respect for students. Bear in mind the example of the students writing in APA format from a few pages back. Be certain you want what you are asking for and be clear about it—perhaps you will get it. But if you don't do those things, most likely you will not get what you wanted.

The next step is to put the task together and see what you have. Pretend to be a student in the class. In fact, pretend to be a couple of different students. First be a student who has achieved the stated goal. How will this student fare? What if he or she has deficits that are unrelated to the goal? Can this cause a failure to perform that will be misleading to you? Now be a student who has marginal ability in skills related to the goal (*the goal, not the task*). How will this student do? Where will he or she encounter problems and will you be able to recognize what those problems are? Next, be a student who has clearly not achieved this goal, but is very good at other aspects of school life, and perhaps who has a lot of support and high expectations from home. Can this student do well on the task without actually having achieved the goal? Finally, be a student who is really struggling. How will this task affect this student? Will it be a source of great frustration or will it provide a learning opportunity? In asking these questions, you have to realize that assessments cannot be all things to all people; nevertheless, these questions are worthwhile in helping you to evaluate what you have.

How Do I Grade and Communicate the Results Back to the Students?

We thought this was so important we devoted a whole chapter to it, Chapter 10. But we know that many of you are saying, "Hey, I'm on this chapter right now. Let's talk about grading here and we can go over it again in Chapter 10." Actually, Chapter 10 looks at the issue somewhat broadly, so it might be useful to look at the issue of grading at a closer level here. Let's consider grading an individual math word problem. There are a number of possibilities. The simplest is to only give credit for a completely correct answer. This seems a bit unfair and is not a practice we endorse. A second approach is to start with full credit for the correct answer, then deduct points as students move away from that correct answer. A small computational error might cost 1 point out of a total of 10. Inappropriately applying an algorithm may cost 2 or 3 points. But what about misconceptualizing the problem, but then working the misconceptualization out properly? Does that receive no credit?

The idea of matching the observed performance to a perfect performance then deducting for weaknesses is often a useful model, but you might want to try turning that around. Start at 0 points and work up, rather than starting at a perfect score and working down. Ask yourself what you are trying to assess with the question or task. If you have a problem that you want to be worth 10 points, how do your objectives for that problem factor out? Is proper conceptualization worth 4 points? Is finding the right algorithm worth 3 points? How much is proper calculation worth? How much is having the right answer worth? You might end up with a scoring algorithm such as this:

1. Five points for understanding what is being asked and setting up the problem properly

2. Three points for applying the proper algorithms

3. Two points for having an answer that is reasonable given the nature of the problem

4. One point deducted for each calculation error

Another approach to this type of problem is to use a rubric, which provides a more generalized and generic approach to scoring. The rubric approach is discussed in detail in Chapter 10, so we won't go over it here.

What About Students Working in Groups?

Students working in groups and sound assessment practice go together like a hand in a very small thimble. It really doesn't work too well. If you are interested in assessing groups, it's fine. If you are interested in assessing individuals, you are pretty much in problem city. When people work in groups, you just don't know who did what and who knows what, and it is therefore hard to assign credit. We have two suggestions for addressing this problem. First, always have an individual component to a group-based task. Then you can grade the individual on that piece. Second, if you are going to use group work, don't have the grade count too much toward the overall course grade and give students opportunities to work in several group settings. And finally, we recommend using groups for instruction more than for assessment. No magic bullets on this one—it's just plain difficult.

In summary, to a great extent we're saying to do what you're doing already. We are recommending some refinements, but if you really want to see the pro, walk down the hall and buy the art teacher a cup of coffee.

CHAPTER 6

Using Multiple Choice and Other Objective Measures

This chapter looks at multiple-choice items and other objective item formats. Multiple-choice items have been the staple of standardized test for decades. They are also popular in high school– and college-level classroom measures, but far less so for kindergarten through eighth grade. In recent years there has been something of a movement away from them at the high school and college levels, although they are still quite popular for assessments in large classes. In this chapter, we will look at when multiple-choice items are useful and when they are not, and we will look at other objective formats, such as short-answer items, as well. What does it mean when a format is *objective*? It usually means that the items can be scored in an objective fashion. While two different people might look at the same essay, performance task, or project differently, they are not likely to score any multiple-choice items differently. Hence, there is no subjectivity in the scoring.

This chapter begins by looking at multiple-choice items, then moves to looking at a format that students and teachers usually call *short answer* and that has come to be called *constructed response* by the measurement field. Technically, a constructed response item is any item that calls for the student to generate a response rather than identify one from a list; for practical purposes, they look just like short-answer items.

When Are Multiple-Choice Items Useful?

We have to admit right up front that we kind of like multiple-choice items. We realize that in this day and age admitting we like multiple-choice items may bring the assessment police knocking at our door, but we'll take that risk. Even though we have a certain fondness for them, we are mindful of useful criticisms of this format. However, there are criticisms of the multiple-choice format that seem to stem more from a religious fervor than from dispassionate consideration. We don't get too worked up over the issue one way or the other. As a wise person said years ago, "Tests are not a fit subject for belief. They are like carpet tacks; they're useful for some things and not for others" (Smith, 1980). So let's look at the multiple-choice format, the pros and cons.

Let's start with the basic idea behind multiple-choice items, then look at some of the criticism. The multiple-choice item was developed not to be the skill that is being measured, but to be a reasonable approximation of the skill. Even the most ardent defender of the multiple-choice format would agree that there are few situations in life that actually look like a multiple-choice item. How often in your job have you been faced with any of these situations?

The Nature of the Multiple-Choice Item

1. You are presented with a clearly stated problem or situation that requires the selection of a correct response.

2. You are presented with a limited number of options, one of which is clearly right, the others, clearly wrong.

3. Your task is to differentiate the right response from the wrong responses.

4. You usually get to find out how well you did in a matter of days or weeks.

Would that life were so straightforward. The major criticism of the multiple-choice format, and a justifiable criticism in our eyes, is that, fundamentally, it does not resemble anything that happens in real life with the possible exception of choosing a dentist.

A second criticism of multiple-choice items is that you can only test fact and recall material (that old devil, mere knowledge). Critics argue that you cannot test higher order thinking skills, application of concepts in novel settings, writing ability, or anything that is actually worthwhile with multiple-choice items. This is simply not true, and we hope to convince you of that a little later in the chapter. Another criticism is that a multiple-choice item is easier than other item formats, because the student doesn't need to construct a response or recall material independently. After all, the answer is there just waiting to be recognized. This isn't true either (remember how "easy" the SAT math section was?). We don't want you to take these ideas on faith, so we will examine the situation. We just wanted to lay all this out up front. The point is that, generally speaking, with a little guidance and practice, a multiple-choice test can be as rigorous, creative, and challenging as other formats and can test skills (even writing proficiency) that represent a higher level of Bloom's taxonomy than simple fact and recall. For us, the question about multiple-choice items does not have to do with whether they can be useful for assessment, but how well they fit with instructional goals. Can you use multiple-choice format to get at skills the way you want to? This poses a serious challenge, and the classroom-based answer to that question might well be "no." However, before you jump to that conclusion, we would like to explore some of the issues.

To begin, we can probably all agree that multiple-choice items are just fine when you *do* have a fact and recall situation. When we were kids, we had to memorize all sorts of lists, like state capitals, symbols on the periodic table of elements, and what the major exported products from all the countries in South America were. For assessing this type of material, the multiple-choice format works fairly well. Short answer is good here as well, but we'll get to that later. Let's look at an example of the format and see what we can do with it:

Multiple-Choice Item 1a

1a. In what year did the Battle of Hastings occur?

    a. 1063
    b. 1064
    c. 1066
    d. 1072

Unless you are a history buff, the correct choice may not be jumping out at you. Of course you might know that something happened in 1066—the Battle of Hastings, the Treaty of Ghent, the signing of the Magna Carta, the year Dick Clark first did a New Year's Eve show, one of those things. Since the question asks for the Battle of Hastings, maybe that's what it is. None of the other numbers rings a bell. But what if the options were changed?

Multiple-Choice Item 1b

1b. In what year did the Battle of Hastings occur?

    a. 1066
    b. 1215
    c. 1492
    d. 1616

These dates all have some meaning in history. Spreading the dates out might make the question more difficult for an adult who has been through a lot of history courses. The original set of options was probably more difficult for a garden-variety high school student who doesn't recognize 1066 as some important date in history. The point here is that playing with the choices allows you to vary both the nature and the difficulty of the item. It also allows you to vary what the assessment tells you about what your students know. For example, in the first set of options, you are testing to find out if students know the exact year of the Battle of Hastings. You are not finding out if they can place the battle historically at all since all of the dates are from the same era. If you used the second set of options and a student picked 1616, you would have to conclude that he or she really didn't understand the eras that the choices represented, or at least not the era the student picked and the era of the correct answer. What type of information is more important for you? Multiple choice allows for gathering a lot of information quickly, and it allows for the ability to go after fairly precise pieces of information, especially if you take the time to look at the wrong answers.

We hear the skeptical reader saying, "But if I made this a short-answer item, I could go after both types of information at the same time. If I simply pose the question like this:

When was the Battle of Hastings? _____

I get all the information I need. I can find out if a student is close and has a general sense of the history we have been talking about, and I can see if he or she knows the exact answer to the question." This is absolutely true. You get a good approximation with the multiple-choice format, but not as good as short-answer in this case. One other small point before leaving this topic: When used for factual recall types of items, multiple choice assesses recognition of the correct answer and short answer assesses recall. If you want students to be able to generate the correct answer, then you probably want short answer. However, how many times have you thought, "I'd know this if it were multiple choice, it's on the tip of my tongue"? Furthermore, multiple-choice items have the distinct advantage of being easy to grade. If you want to get feedback to students as quickly as possible, it's hard to beat the multiple-choice format. It takes more time to write a multiple-choice test than other types of assessments, but grading is much faster, as is turnaround to students.

Let's consider a second example: A multiple-choice item is being used to test the application of a concept in a novel setting. Let's say that you are teaching an introductory psychology course in a high school. You have just completed a unit on Freud, and you want to know if your students understand the differences between the id, the ego, and the superego. Here is an example of a multiple-choice item that asks the students to think about these concepts in an actual setting:

Multiple-Choice Item 2a

2a. It is 4 p.m. and you are going to have dinner at 5 p.m. You are hungry now, and you reach for the cookie jar. Then you put the cookie jar back, telling

yourself that if you have a snack you may spoil your appetite. Freud would
say which of the following most influenced your decision?

> a. id
> b. ego
> c. superego
> d. libido

To arrive at the correct answer (superego), the student must understand the
definition of the superego as the conscience or the location of our guilt feelings when we mess up. This level of understanding must be applied to eliminate a, b, and d as incorrect choices. Contrast this with the following item on
the same material:

Multiple-Choice Item 2b

2b. Which of the following controls our guilt feelings?

> a. id
> b. ego
> c. superego
> d. libido

This item is a straight fact and recall, in which the student simply has to recognize which term fits the definition. Again, you might want to use a different
format here; the point is that the multiple-choice format does a pretty good
job of getting at what we want, particularly, we think, in items like the cookie
jar example.

Excuse us for a minute while we take a quick snack break.

Actually, we believe that even aspects of writing and grammar abilities can
be addressed in a multiple-choice format, although this is an area of strong
contention. But let's say that you have just taught a unit on subject-verb agreement. A multiple-choice item could look like this:

Multiple-Choice Item 3

3.   Which of the following is written correctly?

> a. Each has their own book.
> b. The student has to understand that they will lose a point for each wrong
>   answer.
> c. One of you have made an error.
> d. Either Kalimah or Maria is going to the movies with me.

As with the cookie jar item, in this item students need to understand the concept to select d as the correct choice. The question arises here as to whether
this is actually demonstrating writing ability or just the ability to recognize incorrect subject-verb agreement with pronouns. Three points are worth mak-

ing on this item. First, it does measure an important aspect of what we try to teach students about writing. Second, tests of items like this correlate pretty strongly with tests using written essays by students. Third, no, the ability to write well and the ability to recognize correct grammar are not the same. There are students who will excel at one and not the other—not *many*, but some. In all honesty, there is really one big problem with measuring writing in this fashion—it encourages teachers to teach in this fashion, and that is not what we want. We think we all agree that we want teachers to actually teach students to write and not just to be able to answer editing questions in a multiple-choice format. As Messick (1989) stated so eloquently in an essay on test validity, we must always think about what the consequences of our testing practices are.

Now let's take a look at how a multiple-choice item can address higher-order thinking skills. It would be simple to move to the analytical section of the Graduate Record Exams here, or take an item from the multistate bar examination, but let's stay with examples that relate to what we are interested in, the elementary and secondary level. Imagine an elementary science class that had been working on photosynthesis:

Multiple-Choice Item 4

4. Which of the following would occur if photosynthesis stopped?
    a. Earth's atmosphere would become nearly devoid of gaseous oxygen.
    b. No organisms would be able to exist.
    c. The polar caps would melt, flooding the planet.
    d. Green plants would develop the ability to maintain their functions while brown.

Here, students are required to think about what they know about photosynthesis and how that knowledge relates to each of the possibilities given. In addition to being a useful higher-order task, this item illustrates a situation in which it would be very difficult to tap into the same ability using a short-answer format. Try it. By the way, the answer is a—but you knew that.

We have looked at a number of issues regarding multiple-choice items. We have not, however, addressed the question, "Can't the students just guess and get the answer right?" Well, yes and no, mostly no. Consider a multiple-choice test with five options per item and a student who had no idea what the answer was to any item. The student guesses randomly from among all of the choices.

What are the student's chances of getting all five items right?

1. 1:2 (will either get them all right or not)
2. 1:5 (five choices for each item, so one in five)
3. 1:3,125 (a one out of five chance on each one, so $\frac{1}{5} \times \frac{1}{5} \times \frac{1}{5}$, etc.)
4. I don't really know, but I'm guessing it's 3.

You're right, it's 3 (or 4). The impact of guessing, while it exists, is less than most people think.

Another criticism of multiple-choice testing is that it is easier to cheat on multiple-choice items than other kinds of questions. This is probably true and can be a real problem in some settings. Of course, students can cheat in other formats as well. We're not too expert on this topic, but there is an excellent and entertaining book on the topic by our colleague Greg Cizek (1999), which we highly recommend.

How Do You Write Good Multiple-Choice Items?

So, how *do* you go about writing good multiple-choice items? Here are some guidelines to follow. But first, let's go over some of the jargon so that we're all taking the same language. The question itself is referred to as the stem. The responses are called options, distractors, or responses.

Recommendation List for Writing Multiple-Choice Questions

1. **Make sure each item measures something that you care about.** If an item isn't measuring an important instructional goal at some level, it isn't worth having.

2. **No tricks.** We hated it when teachers tricked us on multiple-choice questions. We still hate it. What on earth is gained by tricking students? If a student gets a question wrong, it is important for you to be able to conclude that the student does not have the requisite ability.

3. **Put all of the information in the stem.** We really like to see the entire problem in the stem. That way the students know what they are working on before they get to the responses. That lets the responses be responses.

4. **Use simple, concise language.** Keep the readability level appropriate to the group you are testing. Using new or difficult words adds to the complexity of the item. Remember, unless you are testing vocabulary, you want to know if the students know the material, not whether the students can figure out what the words in the question mean.

5. **Don't repeat words at the beginning of each option.** Remember, the options should be as concise as possible.

6. **Try to resist using negations or other complications.**

7. **Be careful with the use of "always," "never," "all of the above," "none of the above," and so on.** This is not to say they are never appropriate, but always think about what you are doing before you use them. "All of the above" is almost always a bad idea because if the student knows two of the options are correct, then "all of the above" has to be the right answer. Also, when you start playing around with "a and b," "none of the above," and so on, you run the risk of measuring students' being able to work their way through your question rather than their knowledge of history or science.

8. **Place blanks or omissions at the end of the stem.** As much as possible, if you are going to use a fill-in-the-blank type of item, avoid putting the blank in the middle of the stem. Compare these two items:

Combining two molecules of hydrogen and one molecule of oxygen produces _____.	You get _____ when you combine two molecules of hydrogen and one molecule of oxygen.
a. salt	a. salt
b. water	b. water
c. iron	c. iron
d. gas	d. gas

The item with the blank at the end of the stem is clearer and allows the student to focus on the response in a logical place, that is, in proximity to where it belongs.

9. **Vary the level of thinking involved in your items.** This was basically the whole idea behind Bloom's taxonomy.

10. **Make sure students have enough time.** Go for power, not speed. You don't learn much about what students can and cannot do if they are rushed or don't get to some items.

11. **After you've written the test, go back over it a few days later, imagining that you are the student.** This will let you catch typos, ambiguities, unfair items, and so on.

This is a decent short list of dos and don'ts. If you really want to seriously delve into multiple-choice items, we strongly recommend either of two excellent books on the topic by Thomas Haladyna (1994, 1997).

We're almost done with multiple-choice items—we have two final points before moving on to short answer. First, students really seem to like multiple-choice items. In fact, they typically prefer them to other formats—not all students, but the majority. Second, multiple-choice items are good practice for standardized tests that students have to take. In conclusion, multiple choice are frequently not what we really want for our natural classroom assessment activities, but they do have some redeeming qualities: They allow you to gather a lot of information fairly quickly, students seem to like them, and they are good practice for other, important measures that students have to take.

How Do Short-Answer Items Compare With Multiple-Choice Items?

A lot of people think of multiple-choice items as short-answer items with choices presented, and to a certain extent this is true. However, the presentation of the choices frequently allows you to frame the responses you are looking for and therefore refine the nature and difficulty of the item. For example, consider this short-answer question:

> What title or event is typically associated with William Henry Harrison?

You are looking for "Hero of Tippecanoe," but what if a student writes "President of the United States" or "gave long inaugural address in the cold and rain and died of pneumonia the following month." These are not what you are looking for, but they are reasonable responses to the question. If you provide the following four choices, you can avoid this problem:

     a.   Hero of Tippecanoe

     b.   Old Hickory

     c.   Fire and Brimstone

     d.   Dutch

Now you have framed the question to get at the issue of what Harrison's nickname was.

Having said this, short-answer items are very useful in classroom assessment. They let you assess a lot of information in a relatively short amount of time and with some creativity on your part, you can also look at higher order thinking skills. Short-answer items can vary from items that have a single word or number as the correct answer to items that require several sentences of explanation for an answer. Much longer than several sentences would probably make an item an essay item, but that is a matter of semantics; it doesn't really affect the assessment issue.

How Do I Write Good Short-Answer Questions?

In some respects, it is probably easier to write good short-answer questions than good multiple-choice questions, but it is harder to tell you how to do it since there is such a wide variety of possibilities available. Let's give it a try.

Recommendation List for Writing Good Short-Answer Questions

1. **Start with important instructional outcomes.** The best way to begin to write short-answer questions, or probably any kind of questions, is to be certain you have in mind what you want your students to be able to do. In Chapter 3 we talked about working from instructional goals to instructional activities to assessment. The same idea should hold true here. What are you doing instructionally and how might this relate to finding out how well students are doing?

2. **Refine the general goals into more specific ideas.** Once you have the broad idea, move to more specific topics or aspects that are important for students to know.

3. **Think about the levels of thinking skills in which you are interested.** Try to keep away from asking only knowledge-level questions, especially if higher-level skills such as analysis or generalization are part of your goals.

4. **Pose your questions clearly; be sure to ask for what you want.** Always review your questions to make sure that students will understand exactly what it is you want them to do. Look for other ways they might interpret your questions.

5. **If students are to write more than a word or a phrase, give them an idea of how much writing you want.** If you don't want to read more than 25 words on a topic, tell the students that.

That's a good beginning list of dos and don'ts for short-answer items.

Let's summarize what went on in this chapter. It concerned multiple-choice and short-answer items. We focused fairly heavily on multiple-choice items, as we think they are probably more useful than most teachers think they are. You can really do a lot with multiple-choice items, and they are easy to grade, but you have to remember that the multiple-choice format is almost never exactly what you want. It is an approximation to what you want. We looked at criticisms to multiple-choice testing, those we believe are warranted and those we think are not. Then we presented a list of dos and don'ts for multiple-choice items. We concluded the chapter by touching on the topic of other types of short-answer questions. There is a wide variety of these, and most teachers are fairly familiar with them. Generally speaking—and this is probably true of most assessments—it is absolutely key to be sure that you are measuring important instructional goals, that your questions are stated clearly and directly, and that your students understand what is expected of them.

CHAPTER 7

Using Essays and Reports

In this chapter, we look at two of the most widely used assessment formats in classrooms: essays and reports. Although there are distinct and important differences between essays and reports, their commonalities are important enough to consider them together here. By *essay*, we mean a writing activity, whether done on a test or independently, in which the writing is what is of foremost interest. By *report*, we mean an assignment that includes both a writing component and a research or informational component. Thus, the difference between the two is primarily that a report—for example, a book report, a research report, a report on a project—typically involves research or is based on some information source, and an essay comes primarily from within the individual. Others may want to differentiate essays and reports in some other fashion, and they may have a more useful scheme than this one. We invite them to write a book. If you would like to look at a work exclusively dedicated to assessment in the area of literacy, including writing, we recommend Rhodes (1993).

When Are Essays and Reports the Best Way to Assess?

By their nature, essays and reports are typically solid forms of assessment. The fundamental idea behind Writing Across the Curriculum is that the development of writing skills is so important that it should be emphasized in all subject areas. Practice in writing is practice in thinking. We are basically in favor of writing as an assessment tool. Having said that, we also have to acknowledge that reports and essays may not always be the best forms of assessment. But they are typically so good from an instructional perspective that we may decide to accept some of their limitations. So the question becomes, "When are essays and reports the best way to assess?"

Essays and reports are excellent forms of assessment when you want your students to be in charge of an intellectual activity pretty much from the beginning and you want the form of the assessment to be written. Essays and reports require developing and organizing ideas, working with a sense of audience, taking a project through from beginning to end, and being able to evaluate one's efforts critically. There is a real sense of "putting it all together" when one produces a report on an assignment, or writes an essay on a specific topic. In some respects, you can't go wrong using the essay format on an assessment or requiring a report to be written, but there are certain weaknesses to the format, and for some types of assessment, essays and reports are inefficient, or somewhat inappropriate.

Some areas where you don't want to use essays and reports are obvious. In the sciences and mathematics, frequently the nature of the goal simply doesn't lend itself very well to writing, and in these cases, we don't believe in forcing the issue. Sometimes you just have to get the right answer, and how you feel about having gotten the right answer may not be overwhelmingly useful in the grand scheme of things. There are other not-so-obvious areas where essays are less effective. Essays and reports are not good for assessing achievement of a goal that calls for the accumulation of a lot of information. For example, your class has been studying the continent of Africa, and you want students to be able to identify the countries and their types of government and chief industries. An essay on this information is not going to get you the kind of information about a student's knowledge that a simple objective assessment, such as a short-answer, matching, or multiple-choice test, will. (You could even develop a "quiz show" for this type of assessment. Just be sure that you are getting *good* information on *every* student and not simply having fun.) Assessing a particular skill or ability—the ability to perform long division, for example—*as it is developing* is another area in which essays and reports are not the best choice for assessment.

The critical factor in determining whether to use essays or reports as a form of assessment has to do with the original instructional goal. What is the nature of the goal? Does it lend itself to an essay or report? Can a person turn in a good essay or report and still not have achieved the goal? Can a person have achieved the goal and still not turn in a good essay or report? These are the issues that have to be considered. You must also keep in mind that requiring writing can be a double-edged sword. On one edge, it's almost always good to have students write; on the other edge, your assessment will always be somewhat confounded by how well students write.

What Are Good Questions/Prompts/Tasks/ Assignments for Reports and Essays?

To begin, the requirement should be as good a reflection of the goal as possible. It is hard to get too specific here, as goals vary. But a good practice would be to check back with the goal once the prompt/assignment has been developed and ask yourself, "What does this prompt/assignment require the student to do? What does it allow the student to do? Am I going to get what I need out of the prompt/assignment?" Having said that, you also want to make sure that the prompt/assignment is going to be challenging to students, that it will catch their interest. If you are having trouble framing an assignment or a task, ask for some help from colleagues who you feel are particularly creative. Let's look at an example. Say you were interested in students' understanding the causes of World War I. You've told them that they are going to take an essay test on the causes of World War I and that they will have 45 minutes in class to complete their essay on a specific topic. Now the question becomes, what will be the question? Let's start out with the straightforward approach.

Essay Test on the Causes of World War I

You have 45 minutes to explain the causes of World War I. Be sure to include both the long-term causes and the immediate causes. Try to formulate well-structured and complete paragraphs and make your essay as interesting to the reader as possible. A small portion of your grade will relate to grammar and punctuation, but spelling will not be counted. I am looking for a final essay in the range of 200 to 300 words. Do your best and good luck.

Let's see what we have. This is a clear statement of what is expected of the student and seems straightforward to us. It strikes a pretty good balance between too vague and too detailed, although one might argue that it could be somewhat more specific. It allows students to lay out their knowledge of the topic. However, it is pretty mundane from the perspective of the student. You are likely to get back whatever was in the textbook and supplementary materials and what was covered in class. This may be exactly what you want, and in that case, it's OK to go ahead with something like this. Or you may be thinking, "I guess this is all right, but it seems kind of dry. I'm not certain I'd want to be doing this. How can I make this a little bit more exciting or interesting?" You might also want to take into consideration that you will be grading 25 or so of these puppies, so you might want to put a little interest factor into it for your own sake. Let's look at a possible revision of this assessment.

> ### What Really Caused World War I?
>
> Some people have argued that the murder of Archduke Ferdinand was the cause of World War I. Others argue that this was simply the event that started the war and that it would have occurred anyway. For this essay, you are to take one side of the argument or the other and present the case for that side. It will be necessary to think about what the counterarguments are and address them in your essay. Remember that you are making an argument here, so you want your writing to be strong and persuasive. It doesn't matter which side you take. You will have 45 minutes to complete your essay, which should be about 200 to 300 words in length. Be careful with grammar and punctuation, as they will be a small part of your grade. Spelling will not be counted as part of the grade on this essay.

Now there's a bit of a hook to the question, perhaps a bit more for the students to sink their teeth into. It should also make for somewhat more interesting reading on your part. We need to check this formulation to make sure that it really fits with the instructional objective as well as the first formulation did and that the format is not going to present a disadvantage to any of the students. Never being ones to leave well enough alone, we're going to try one more time on this question to see if we can make it even more interesting.

> ### Archduke Ferdinand Assassinated! What Happens Now?
>
> You are the editorial writer for the *Sarajevo Sovereign Times Weekly* newspaper. Archduke Ferdinand was murdered two days ago, and you have to write an analysis of the situation for your newspaper. You have the distinct advantage of being able to look at the situation from eight decades later—so you really know what happened. Try to put yourself in the shoes of someone who knows about the politics of the situation (a newspaper editorial writer) and is right in the situation as it happens. Consider some of these questions. Does it really look like war? Why? What are the various factions that oppose one another? What might be done to prevent war at this point? What should the average citizen of Sarajevo do? Using the 45 minutes of the class period, write an analysis of the situation for your newspaper. Make your analysis 200 to 300 words long. Remember that your audience is composed of people who are eager to understand the ramifications of what is going on and are worried about their futures. Should you be reassuring or give them an honest assessment of a dire situation? Grammar and punctuation will count for a small part of your grade, but spelling will not. Good luck.

The students have now been put into a real situation. They have to think about form as much as content. This assignment may make demands on students that can't be met, particularly by younger students. It may also push the assignment too far away from the original goals of understanding the proximal and distal causes of World War I. So, should this assignment be used or not? That's really up to your professional judgment. Can your students handle it? Will it cause them to become more engaged in the assignment and bring out their best, or will it cause confusion in some students that you wish to avoid? Again, you have to be the judge of this. What we want to emphasize with this progression of assignments on the same theme is that there is a lot of latitude and potential for creativity in developing tasks for students. If you are not the creative type, get some help from friends who are. Once you have explained what the goal is and laid out the basics, anyone can help you brainstorm on this.

Although the exact nature of this task was varied from one setting to the next, some things remained the same. Time limits, word limits, and some notion of what would and would not count as part of the grade on the assignment were included in all three versions. This is consistent with our argument that you can't get from students what you don't ask for. More specifically, we like the notion of time and/or word limits. Some teachers we have talked to don't like them, preferring the notion that a writing assignment should take however long it takes the student to complete it. Not an unreasonable position in our minds, but we prefer targets to be set. In real life, targets are set for writing all the time. For example, we had a page goal for this book set by the publisher. And one could write a book on the causes of World War I—in fact, many have—but for this assignment, 200 to 300 words sufficed. Students need to know if they should spend their time just getting as much information down on paper as possible or if they should present less information and spend their time crafting really good paragraphs.

How Many Essays Should Be on a Test, and How Long Should They Be?

One of the choices that has to be made on essay exams is how many essays should be on the exam and how long should they be? Here the issue is basically one of how many different concepts need to be assessed and how much time is available for the assessment. Let's say that you have eight different areas of knowledge or concepts that you would like to know about from the students and 40 minutes to do the assessment. How should this task be approached? Well, at first blush, one might say that eight essay questions of

5 minutes each would be a good approach, and it may be. But we should consider some other possibilities as well.

Possibilities for an Essay Test With Eight Topics and 40 Minutes

1. Have students write eight essays, spending 5 minutes on each. This is the most obvious possibility and allows for equal coverage of all eight topics. The downside is that none of the topics will get a very extensive look.

2. Have students choose four topics from among the eight listed and write for 10 minutes on each. This allows each student to play to his or her strength and provides you with a more in-depth picture of ability. However, it might lead you to overestimate student knowledge, since students may be able to avoid one or two areas where they are particularly weak.

3. Have students write one extensive essay on one topic (roughly 20 minutes) and seven short essays (roughly 3 minutes each) on the other topics. This allows you to check for knowledge on all of the topics and to see if students can work in depth in the area in general by having them do so on one topic.

The key here is not to limit yourself to one way of looking at the problem. There are a variety of possibilities available.

On an Essay Test, Should Topics Be Communicated in Advance?

This is an excellent question—we're glad we asked it. First, there are several different ways to provide topics in advance. You could provide the exact question or questions in advance. You could provide a list of topics and tell students that a certain number of those topics would be picked. You could provide general areas of the topics and tell students that questions will be developed from that list. There are other possibilities as well.

What would be the advantages and the disadvantages of providing topics in advance? Looking first on the plus side, if topics are provided in advance, then students will work on the topics that have been given to them. This would cause students to work on just what we wanted them to work on. Our assessment activity is working in the service on instruction. This is a powerful argument for providing the topics. Furthermore, students are not surprised by what they find on the assessment and don't feel like they have been spending time studying topics that are then not included on the assessment. If they are given eight topics and told they will be tested on four, they tend to feel like the time spent on the four not tested to be wasted time. If they do not know what will be on the test, then topics that they study for that are not on the test are more likely to be thought of as not productive. Giving students knowledge of what they are responsible for gives them a sense of control over their academic lives. We all like to be in control of things that are important to us.

On the negative side of the equation concerning giving students topics in advance, doing this will limit their studying to those topics that are given. Furthermore, if specific questions are given, you run into trouble with the idea that someone other than the student may be generating the response. To some extent, this is always a problem when work is done at home rather than at school. You need to decide what you want students doing in preparation for the assessment and what will provide you with the information that you desire.

What Do Good Assignments for Reports Look Like?

Our focus thus far has concentrated on essay assessments, but this chapter concerns writing for reports as well. We have differentiated reports as those assignments that involve the gathering of information and reporting on it in some fashion. It might be a research report, a book report, or a report on a project or activity. What would a good assignment of this type look like? Reports are naturally part instruction, part assessment. Therefore, it is critical to make sure that the report accurately reflects the instructional goals.

Research reports begin with what you want the students to do. Do you want them to choose and develop the topic, or will that be provided? If students are to develop their own topics for the report, is this something they have had practice in? How much support and approval are you going to provide? After the topic has been developed or assigned, students have to seek out the information that will form the basis of the report. What options are available to them? Are the options going to be the same for all students, or can students go beyond a standard list if they so desire?

Following the development of the topic and the determination of what resources are available for students, the nature of the final product has to be specified. What is it exactly that you are looking for? What is the information base that will form the basis for the report? How long should this report be? Should it be typed (word-processed) or is a handwritten report permissible? Are there specific issues that need to be addressed in the report? What is the penalty for turning the project in late? Later in the book these topics are discussed in more detail. For now, we want to emphasize that these issues need to be addressed.

Let's look at a couple of possibilities here.

What Is a Black Hole?

Your assignment is to explore the idea of black holes and report on your findings. We need to know what black holes are, what they do, where they are, and what they have to do with us. Also, we need to know who first proposed the idea of a black hole? You must have at least four references for your work. One of these may be an encyclopedia, and one may be from the Internet. Your final report should be at least two typewritten double-spaced pages long, and no longer than four pages. You should pay attention to punctuation, grammar, and spelling. You will receive a letter grade for this assignment, and it will count as 20% of your grade for the marking period. If you are having trouble finding references, please see me about it before December 10. Your final report is due on December 17. You will be penalized a half-grade for each day it is late, so be sure you are on time with this assignment.

Living in the Time of the Great American Depression

We have been studying the Depression for the past four weeks. Now we are going to look at the human side of this American tragedy. Your assignment is to find someone in your family or neighborhood to interview who lived through the Depression. I have some people who have volunteered to be interviewed if you cannot find anyone, but I really want you to talk to someone you know, if possible. Ask them about what life was like for their family. How did they make it through the Depression? What was day-to-day life like? What did they do to earn money? to get food and shelter? How did they keep their spirits up? Once you have conducted your interview, write an essay that takes this personal information and combines it with what you have learned in the unit so far. Find a theme that will allow you to effectively blend the information from these two sources. For example, the theme could be family life, making resources stretch farther, or helping out neighbors. After you have decided on a theme, please check with me to get it approved. Your final report should be four, word-processed, double-spaced pages long (at least three and a half, not more than five). I will be looking for an interesting and insightful essay that "puts a human face" on this terrible time for America. I will also be looking carefully at good paragraph development, sentence structure, grammar, punctuation, and spelling. This should be a very professional-looking report. Your report is due on February 19. There will be a half-grade penalty for each day the report is late. Let's get started on this right away.

Both of these assignments appear to be fairly explicit, providing good direction to students who will be working on them. For each of these assignments, some more specificity on grading might be made available to the students, particularly for students in earlier grades. At the high school level, this amount of specificity should be sufficient. One thing that is not covered explicitly here is how much assistance is permissible in completing the assignment. It is assumed for each of these that students will work on their own. You may want to make that statement on the assignment sheet directly.

Before leaving essays and reports, let's talk for a bit about what we want to do with regard to scoring these efforts. There are several possibilities for approaching this issue. The first approach would be to develop a scoring rubric that is somewhat generic in nature, as is discussed in Chapter 10. Another approach would be to develop a system that analyzes aspects of the essay or the report and scores it according to these aspects. This is often referred to as "analytical scoring." From our perspective, analytical scoring evolves most logically from instructional goals. To develop a scoring system, it is necessary to ask why the assessment was developed the way it is, and what we want to accomplish with it. If you look at the last six lines of the Great American Depression assignment, you find what the goals are for the assignment. In this assignment, you are looking for an interesting and insightful essay that focuses on the human side of the Depression. You are also looking for good paragraph development, along with good sentence structure, grammar, and punctuation. You want the report to look professional. Let's see if we can translate this into a scoring system:

1. Overall content of the report. Did the report engage the reader? Did it make the reader think about the human side of the Depression? Was there something original or insightful in the essay? Up to 60 points.

2. Paragraph development. Did the essay have strong, clear paragraphs, with each paragraph focused on a single topic or idea that was developed fully? Up to 25 points.

3. Sentence structure and grammar. Did the essay have complete sentences with proper subject-verb agreement and appropriate use of antecedents? Was there variety in the sentence structure? Up to 15 points.

Note that this scoring system focuses almost exclusively on the writing ability of the student. If you are interested more in the substantive issues involved in the Depression, the instructions should explain that you have such an interest. You are free to score essays and reports as you will, but it is important to make certain that the scoring reflects your goals and your instructional activities and that students understand clearly what your expectations are.

Essays and reports are forms of assessment that we believe are very helpful and productive in the instructional process. They are useful in a wide variety of settings, and since they provide good practice for writing skills, they are justifiable even in some settings where another approach might provide somewhat better information. It is important to take into consideration that writing skills, or the lack thereof, may negatively impact the quality of the inference you draw about student abilities. We believe that essay questions or prompts and report assignments should flow naturally from instructional goals. We also believe that it is important to be explicit about what students are to do and what will count and not count toward a grade. And finally, students should know what resources are available to them and what resources are not available.

CHAPTER 8

Incorporating Affective and Related Ideas

In this chapter, we are going to look at the affective side of assessment. By this we mean ideas such as counting participation as part of a grade, assessing for working up to one's potential, and improvement over the course of a marking period or from one period to the next (although the latter two notions aren't technically affective, they seem to fit in nicely here). This is a rather difficult area for many teachers. Opinions vary widely and are often deeply held by teachers. We have seen more than one vigorous debate in the middle of an in-service workshop or in a teachers' lounge over the issue of counting participation as part of a grade. We'll look at various opinions on the topic and provide what we hope will be some useful ways of looking at the issue.

Is Counting Participation Fair?

In some respects, this is the heart of the issue: Is counting participation fair? This is where two of the bedrock notions that we have been promoting in this book come into conflict. To begin, if you revisit your instructional goals for your classroom or course, you are unlikely to find classroom participation among them. Your goals are likely to concern the development of reading skills, the ability to find patterns in historical events, or an appreciation of how physics is related to everyday life. But you are not likely to find something like, "The student will participate in classroom discussions, offer to answer difficult questions, and help peers who haven't mastered a given skill." So from the perspective of instructional goals, it looks like participation shouldn't count toward a grade since it isn't one of our instructional goals.

The other side of the coin has to do with assessment enhancing instruction. Here the argument runs roughly as follows. If you do not reward participation in the classroom, you are less likely to get it, and the quality of classroom life will suffer. Children learn more in active and participatory classrooms;

therefore the assessment system should reward such participation. After all, as was pointed out earlier in the book, it's better to have a great instructional program and an OK assessment system than a great assessment system and an OK instructional system. So there.

In a perfect world, we wouldn't count participation as part of the assessment system, as it typically wouldn't be one of our instructional objectives. Class participation is a teaching issue, not an assessment issue, and given our druthers, we would like to rely on extrinsic motivation as little as possible in instruction. Last time we checked, however, nobody teaches in a perfect world. Most people teach in real schools with real kids. If participation can be successfully encouraged by having it count as part of the grading system, it seems a small price to pay to enhance our instructional efforts. So this is where we are on this issue: If counting participation really seems to be an effective instructional tool, it would be foolish not to use it. But at the same time, we would have it count for as little of the total grading process as possible, and we would develop a system for counting it that takes into account the variety of problems associated with doing it, which we get to next.

Is It Really Participation That We Want?

Active participation sounds like a good thing, but is it always? Take the phrase "active participation" and apply it to your mother-in-law in determining your vacation plans for next summer. OK, that wasn't fair, and we're sure your mother-in-law is a perfectly wonderful person, but at the same time, you get our point. If you're not convinced, let us play out an interaction that we always like to engage in when doing inservice work on assessment and grading activities. Imagine a consultant, whom we'll call Jeff, conducting a workshop and a teacher at the workshop named Joan. The interaction usually goes something like this.

Jeff: Who uses participation as part of the grading system in your classroom?

(This usually gets somewhere between half and two thirds of the hands. Often, participation goes down as the grade level goes up. Also, math instruction tends to use participation less than other subjects do. Hardest to predict are social studies teachers, who seem to be either ardently in favor of counting participation or adamantly opposed to it.)

OK, Joan, you're hand is up. Do you mind if we explore how you count participation as part of your grading system?

Joan: No problem.

Jeff: Super. Can you give us a quick overview of how you use participation to count in your grading system.

Joan: Basically, I use participation to move students who are on the cusp between two grades either up to the next or not, depending on how much they have participated in class. Also, if a student has been an excellent participator, I may give them a half-grade boost.

Jeff: Would you lower a student's grade if he or she had not been participating in class?

Joan: Do you mean if a student had a B-minus would I drop it to a C-plus?

Jeff: Exactly.

Joan: No, I wouldn't do that.

Ed: I would. *(Ed is a social studies teacher.)*

Jeff: Thanks for your participation, Ed. OK, I'm going to continue with Joan now. Let's say you ask a question, and Mary raises her hand and offers up an answer. It's not anywhere near correct, but it's a good faith effort. Does that count in your class as good participation?

Joan: Absolutely.

Jeff: And would you give Mary some indication that she had participated well?

Joan: Probably, depending on the situation. I wouldn't always do it, but most times I would.

Jeff: Excellent. Now let's say a little later you ask a question and once again Mary offers up an effort, and again it's wrong. Still good participation?

Joan: You betcha.

Jeff: Now, Jack is noticing that Mary is getting rewarded for her efforts even though she doesn't get any of the answers right. Jack is no fool, and this seems like a decent way to improve his grade, so he starts raising his hand and offering answers, even though he usually has no idea what he is talking about and knows it. Good participation?

Joan: Well, at some point you have to draw a line here. I don't want people throwing out answers just to suck up participation points. This isn't usually a problem for me.

Jeff: How do you know that Mary wasn't playing the same game that Jack was? Wasn't the behavior fairly similar?

Joan: It may seem so, but I know what I'm doing as a teacher. This is where my 15 years of experience comes in.

Jeff: OK, now let's turn to Katie. Katie is a pretty good student who usually hangs out between a B and an A in your class, but she is painfully shy. In the four months you have had her in class, she has yet to raise her hand. She will respond when you call on her, but she speaks very softly and uses the minimal number of words to not be impolite in responding to your question. How does she fare in your participation system?

Joan: Well, I wouldn't want to penalize her, but I guess she wouldn't get the extra credit for participating if she didn't participate.

Jeff: And finally, what about Mark who believes he participated quite well, but you don't remember it that way?

Joan: Sometimes students *do* see this differently than I do.

We'll end the dialogue now because a few useful points have been made that need to be examined. Four points to be exact. The first point is that not all participation is helpful. In one of our inservice presentations on assessment and grading, one of the teachers in the group came up with what we thought was a brilliant observation. Putting the point succinctly she said, "Not all participation is contribution." What you want is for students to contribute to the workings of the class. Putting one's hand up and asking, "Is this going to be on the test?" isn't a contribution to the class. In fact, it's a nuisance. On the other hand, bringing an article from a magazine that pertains to what is being discussed in class is a contribution, but it's not participation in a class discussion sense. If we reconceptualize participation as contribution, it does two things for us. First, it allows us to differentiate between talk that contributes and talk that does not, and second, it allows for a wide range of other behaviors to be counted as contributory. It is a small change in vocabulary, but it allows for a more productive way to look at the issue. As a teacher you can say, "here is a list of things that I feel contribute to our class. If you don't find one way that you feel you are comfortable with, try another."

What About Students Who Are Shy or Whose Culture Discourages Speaking Up?

The second point we want to look at from the dialogue above is the situation of the student who is shy, or whose cultural background has led him or her to be reluctant to make contributions in class. Students are not active participants for other reasons as well. A few years back, the fifth-grade science teacher of one of our children asked why Ben didn't seem to like science class. Now, Ben loved science class and thought the science teacher was truly outstanding. The teacher said that Ben never raised his hand in class. When Ben was asked about this, he said, "Oh, Dad, Mr. Mignano knows that I know the answers. I don't put my hand up so that he can find out if the other kids know the answers."

Ben's case may be unusual, but the problem is that you often don't really know why a student who doesn't contribute to the discussion in the class behaves in that way. Is it lack of interest, shyness, cultural differences, laziness, lack of confidence in the ability to speak English? We need to look at two issues. First, we need to think about why students are not participating and what might be done to encourage more participation. How can we bring out the students who are currently too shy to speak or who think they have nothing to contribute? With students who have cultural differences, we probably need to speak to parents to make sure that our efforts are not in conflict with their desires. The second aspect of this issue is to make sure that there are a variety of ways that a student can make a contribution to class. We can also let students know how they are doing in this regard so that they are not surprised by their grades.

How Can I Make Sure That I'm Not Playing Favorites?

The third point brought out by the dialogue concerns the danger of playing favorites. In our discussions with students, this is an area of substantial concern for them. How can you be sure that the students whose grades are being raised by half a grade are really the ones making the best contributions and are not simply your favorites in some fashion? Furthermore, even if you are being fair, how can you guard against the perception that you are not being fair? We have some suggestions. Make it clear to the class at the beginning of the year what you mean by contributing to the class, why it is important, and how you are going to keep track of it. Having done this at the beginning of the year, it is also helpful to reinforce what you are doing at regular intervals so that students can pick up on what is going on. It's important to say, "Thanks, Kaitlin, that was really helpful," or "Duane brought in this great article about what we were talking about yesterday." Finally, it is useful at times to look at your student roster and ask yourself, "Am I really being fair to all of the students? Are there students here whom I really don't like and are they being treated unfairly because of this? Who deserves a fresh start, a clean slate in how I look at them? Can I look at Danny's behavior in a new light and try harder to see the positive side?" We know this sounds a little corny or Pollyannaish, but we would recommend just giving it a try with one or two students on a pilot basis and see how it works out.

How Should Student Classroom Participation Be Counted?

The fourth point that came up in the dialogue, perhaps a little bit obliquely, was the notion of how to keep track of who is making a contribution and who isn't. What we want to get is a system of record keeping that is fair and consistent and that doesn't require a whole lot of time. We would encourage a somewhat more systematic record keeping than just your own recollection about who was contributing and who wasn't. Life is probably too busy for you to keep track of this on a daily basis, but a weekly basis might not hurt. You could set up a system where you could code a plus (+) at the end of the week for each student whom you felt had done a good job of making a contribution. You might even want to make a note of what it was. This is helpful not only to you, but it is great for parent/teacher conferences, a topic that gets its own chapter shortly. Again, there is a trade-off between the time spent keeping records now and the quality of information you have for making decisions later. Before leaving this topic, we have to mention a brilliant idea we heard at one of our workshops for rewarding contribution.

Rewarding Contributions to the Class: *Biology Bucks*

Probably the most innovative idea we have ever heard for rewarding class participation was the concept of Biology Bucks presented by a high school biology teacher whose name we have unfortunately lost. Should he see this, we would be glad to give him full credit in the second edition. For now we'll call him Mr. Mendel. Mr. Mendel wanted to reward students who contributed to the class and he wanted it to be a fair system without his having to do a lot of record keeping. So he invented Biology Bucks. He began by cutting out a small picture of his face and sticking it on a dollar bill where George Washington usually is. He then made a whole lot of photocopies of the dollar. (We note that this is probably a violation of federal law, and we definitely do not endorse such practices. If you are going to do something like this, we would recommend play money of some sort. But it is important that it be hard for students to duplicate your bucks or whatever you call them—Lit Loot, perhaps. Whatever you do, do not violate federal law as a regular classroom practice, or even occasionally, for that matter).

Mr. Mendel kept the Biology Bucks in his desk drawer, and whenever anybody in the class did something that was meritorious (participating usefully, answering a particularly difficult question, helping out a classroom, bringing in a biological specimen, etc.), Mr. Mendel would announce, "That's worth a Biology Buck!" The student would then go up to Mr. Mendel's desk, whereupon he would pull out a Buck, write the student's name on it, sign it, and give it to the student.

We know what you're thinking. You're thinking, "And that was rewarding?" We're not done. After Mr. Mendel told us this, we said, "And that was rewarding?" "No," he replied, "I'm not done yet." The next part of the system was brilliant, even though we don't agree with all of it. In Mr. Mendel's system, whenever he gave a test, graded a lab, or administered other assessment type activities, he would score it numerically on a 100-point basis, then convert the score into a letter grade in his grade book. It was the letter grades that ultimately worked toward the grade in the course. (That was the part we don't like; we prefer to see the number grades used until the final averaging.) At any rate, if a student got an 88 on a test, the student would receive a B or B+, unless the student happened to have two Biology Bucks. She could then trade the two Biology Bucks in to bump her score up to a 90, which would be an A. Students could use their Biology Bucks whenever they felt the need to do so. They could not trade them, however.

Consider the advantages. First, Mr. Mendel has no record keeping to worry about. Second, he immediately and publicly rewards the behavior he wants to encourage. Third, there is an element of fun in the system that contributes to the overall functioning of the class. With the small exception that we don't like recording numerical grades as letter grades (because a 90 becomes the same as a 100, whereas an 89 becomes the same as an 80, when in fact the 89 is almost indistinguishable from the 90), we think this idea has a lot of potential. One more thought before we move on: In response to hearing about this, one teacher said, "But you are using extrinsic motivation with the students to get them to participate when intrinsic motivation is clearly better." An interesting point, but not one limited to Biology Bucks. If you count participation/contribution as part of a grade, you are already using extrinsic motivation; Biology Bucks is just an interesting way to implement the idea.

What About Students Who Are Working As Hard As They Can or Up to Their Potential?

One of the most vexing problems we deal with as educators is that students do not all have the same abilities and talents, do not all work with the same diligence and enthusiasm, and do not all come from the same background in terms of family support. Of course, if they did, life in classrooms might get pretty boring, but the point here has to do with the effort component in the assessment equation. What do we do with students who seem to be working as hard as they can and still seem to be "getting nowhere?" If a student's paper appears to show a sincere effort to complete the assignment, yet falls pretty much short of the mark in terms of the goals we have, what do we do? Do we factor effort into the grade that we give for that paper? What about another student, whose paper does not show much in the way of effort but meets the requirements because the student has substantially more ability in this area than other students?

This is a tough one. It is so tough, in fact, that we almost left it out of the book. That didn't seem fair, however. So here is our best shot at the issue and pretty much how we feel about it. We use the concept of instructional goals as our touchstone. Whenever we face a difficult problem, we go back to the idea of goals, which is why they are so important to us in the first place. Two questions need to be answered here. First, do you have the same instructional goals for the two students? If you do, then you should grade them on the same standards. If you do not, then you can grade them on different standards. In most cases you have the same goals for all students (with the exception of classified students, a subject we deal with in chapter 12). Second, do your instructional goals relate to how hard students work, or do you individuate students in some fashion, such as saying they should grow as much as they can individually? If you do, then you can set different standards of performance for different students, but this is a bit tricky and can get you into situations you might best want to avoid.

There are two basic problems here. The first has to do with determining students' potential and the second has to do with comingling affect and cognition. First, let's look at the issue of potential. It often seems to us as teachers that as we get to know our students, we get an idea of what they can do and what they cannot do. We feel that we therefore know what is a good effort on a piece of work for a particular student and what is less of an effort. This is human nature. But it is also a trap. It is a trap because we are almost certainly wrong with at least a few of our students, which results in our expectations being too high or too low for those students. It is not at all difficult to come up with examples of misperceptions of students we have had over the years. It is one of the reasons that we believe in assessment. A well-constructed and fairly graded assessment gives everyone the same opportunity to show what he or she can do. It doesn't matter if you dress nicely, have concerned parents, smile a lot, or work well with others. An objective assessment is just that: objective.

The question that needs to be posed with regard to the first issue is: "Who am I to determine what this student's potential is? " If we believe we know what a student can do, we have a strong tendency to attribute work that is not up to the student's par to lack of effort. If a student outperforms our expectations, we are likely to congratulate that student for making a good effort. We are even likely to turn that B into an A to encourage the student to keep up the good work. But where do our expectations come from, and do we change them in the light of new information? (In your own schooling, did you ever have a teacher or a professor who didn't realize how bright you were, or who thought you were being lazy when, in fact, you were doing the best that you could?) Try this exercise on your next assessment. After you have collected the assessments (tests, papers, projects, whatever), go to your roster and guess how well each student is going to do. If it is a test, write down the percent correct you expect each student to get. Now go ahead and grade the test, then write down the actual percent correct next to your estimates. Ask these questions:

1. Did the class overall do as well as I expected, worse, or better? (Was the estimated average the same as the actual average?)

2. Are there any students who did a lot better than I expected?

3. Are there any students who did a lot worse than I expected?

We've done this ourselves, and we have had teachers do it. What we find fairly consistently is that teachers are generally pretty good at guessing the overall class average, but that there are almost always students whose scores surprised them. Interestingly, the discrepant scores are usually attributed to strong or weak efforts on the parts of the students on this particular assessment. There is a real tendency to think of students as having a certain amount of ability and that specific performances are a function of that amount of ability and the level of effort that a student puts forth on a particular assessment. Furthermore, there is a tendency to think of the ability level as something that is not in the control of the student, but that the effort level is. Good effort in relation to ability is almost always rewarded, and poor effort is criticized (or sometimes ignored). What is interesting here is that the students may or may not have a notion of what their level of ability is, but they do tend to know when they have put out a good effort and when they haven't. Often, the comments from the teacher, which frequently relate perceived effort to perceived ability, are out of synch with the effort the student feels he or she has put forward.

Our recommendation is to try to keep from making generalizations about student ability, especially if it is not necessary to do so. Try to keep focused on the assessment at hand, and be continually open to revising what you think about your students. Ability is not fixed, not innate, and not unidimensional. We all have things we are good at and enjoy and things in which we are less accomplished. We recommend keeping your focus on what you have from the student, whether it is good work according or not to the goals you have and the progress that has been made toward those goals, and not worrying about whether this or that fourth-grade student shows more or less promise to become a writer, a lawyer, or a doctor.

The second issue has to do with mixing affect and cognition. We've actually touched on this somewhat already, so we'll treat it a bit more briefly than the difficult issue we just discussed. The basic idea is to focus on what you have in front of you in terms of student performance and avoid making judgments about students' abilities based on that information. If a student gets a

73 on a test and it is 10 points higher than any other score the student has gotten so far, or if a paper that the student wrote is substantially better than previous papers, then this is clearly improvement, and improvement is good. It's also the objective fact. As teachers, we're pleased with this. We may even be proud of the student. A comment such as "John, this shows real improvement" would seem appropriate here. But what about the comment, "I'm really proud of the effort you put into this." You may be really proud of this effort and the student may be as well. But imagine that this student sits next to a student who got a 78 after having previously gotten nothing lower than a 97. What kind of comment goes there? How about something like, "Mary, you really slipped up on this. Come see me about it." Or perhaps, "Mary, this is clearly less than I expect of you." Just to play this out all the way, let's say Mary and John are good friends and always compare their work. What do these comments say to John? How about, "John, a 73 is about as good as you can probably do in this class, but since Mary is a heck of a lot smarter than you, I am upset when she gets a 78, which is actually a really low grade." So what should we do? Should we never make comments on student papers? Should our classes be affect free? Should we grade papers like robots or computers? Hey, lighten up. Our recommendation is simple: Be encouraging and optimistic, focus on the facts, and try to avoid sweeping judgments.

What About Students Who Make a Big Improvement?

Some students show a dramatic improvement over the course of a marking period, or from one marking period to another. Others sometimes show a decline. As advocates of our students, we want to celebrate the improvements and look for root causes of the declines. We have never heard ourselves say, "Jack made a really big improvement this semester over last semester, I wonder what's wrong." Big improvements are cause for celebration. The one thing we would be reluctant to do is to overgrade a student because he or she is on the incline. This student is doing well enough objectively. There are plenty of rewards in the objective facts of the matter. At the same time, we would not discount earlier performance because a student isn't doing well now. Declines are a cause for concern and a legitimate cause for exploring what the problem might be. If we have seen students do well and now they are not, then it is likely that something is wrong. We need to remember that we are not social workers or psychologists in the classroom, but some level of inquiry is usually appropriate. Generally speaking, we think that the responses students get on their assessments that are assessment focused are usually reward or correction enough, and we recommend that comments involving more general judgments about students should be used sparingly.

To sum up our considerations on the affective side of assessment, we think that the idea of participation should be refined into the concept of contribution and that counting it as part of a student's grade is probably useful in encouraging a more positive classroom environment. We are not particularly enamored of it as an assessment because it usually is not related to our goals for our students' achievement. But since instruction takes precedence over assessment, it's an idea we can live with. We do recommend trying to be objective about using contribution as part of the grade. We are also a little bit leery about making judgments about student ability and student effort. We prefer to stay away from sweeping judgments where possible and to communicate to students about their progress as it is objectively seen on their assessments.

CHAPTER 9

Preparing Students for Assessments

This chapter concerns the preparation of students for assessments. It's a bit of a touchy topic these days in the field of education in general and the field of assessment in particular. People are particularly concerned about the kinds of test preparation that precede standardized testing, especially what is called high stakes standardized testing (see, for example, Guskey, 1994). The concern centers on the issue of what is proper preparation and what is just teaching students isolated skills in artificial formats that happen to be on the test. Our primary focus in this chapter concerns standardized assessment, but we'll also look at preparing students for the assessments that you develop and give as part of classroom instruction.

What Is Teaching to the Test, and Is It Necessarily Bad?

"Teaching to the test" is one of those phrases that just sounds bad on the face of it. It's like "tax and spend," "mere knowledge," and "daytime TV." Even though on reflection we're not certain that something can "sound bad on the face of it," you get our drift. So what is the deal with teaching to the test? If the test is the ability to write a report, sing an aria, read a technical document, calculate an integral, paint a landscape, or perform an experiment, why wouldn't we want to teach to the test, at least to some degree? How different are regular teaching and teaching to the test (Nitko, 1989)? Where does one cross the line from what is appropriate and acceptable to what is borderline cheating or beyond? The problem takes a bit of explanation, but it is worth the time and effort.

A Brief and Selective History of Testing

A long time ago in a land far away teachers taught their students as they best saw fit. In some of the grades, students would take a standardized measure such as the Iowas or the Californias and the results would be used to see how the school was doing in general. The results would not be reported in the local paper, student-level analysis was frowned on, and nobody was denied a high school diploma because of their test results. Also, you could get a Coke from a machine for a dime, people watched television commercials featuring a beaver selling toothpaste called "Ipana," and blue jeans were not allowed in school. Those days are gone. What has replaced them are standardized tests that are given every year to every student, the results of which are published down to the school level in front-page newspaper articles that decry the lack of achievement in certain schools. And students who have completed all of their high school course work successfully might still be denied a diploma because they cannot pass the high school graduation test. Also, Coke is a dollar from the machine, you can watch commercials for products that couldn't be displayed in public in the 1950s, and nothing but blue jeans are worn in school.

Societal trends aside, we exist in an era in which student testing and the rigorous standards associated with testing seem to be the educational position of choice amongst politicians. Test scores have become the coin of the realm in education, and with that, concerns about how to get students to do well on the tests have risen as well. School districts, schools within districts, and teachers within schools are being evaluated on the basis of their students' test scores with little consideration being given to the multitude of factors that comprise student achievement. With the greatly increased emphasis on test scores comes greater pressure on educators to do well, and with that greater pressure comes a tendency to focus solely on the test score at hand. That is where the trouble begins. Let's look at the standardized tests for a minute.

Just as standardized tests have been extolled by politicians as a powerful lever for getting schools to "do their job," the tests have been castigated by their opponents as artificial, biased, time-consuming distortions of the educational process. So what are they really?

A Brief Self-Assessment on Standardized Tests

1. Standardized tests are
   a. A fair and objective mechanism for determining how well students, teachers, school districts, states, and nations are doing in achieving their educational goals

      b. The work of the devil
      c. A reasonable approach to assessing student progress that has got-
         ten somewhat out of hand in recent years
      d. Seriously, the work of the devil

2. In a well-constructed essay, tell how you feel about your answer to
   Question 1.

So, what are the right answers? The right answers are (c), which is always
the first right answer in a multiple-choice test, and "Not too bad, thanks for
asking." Generally speaking, as teachers we would like to have some idea of
how well our students are doing and wouldn't really object to seeing how well
they are doing compared to other students—it provides a type of standard or
contrast. If we work with students who face a lot of challenges in learning, we
don't expect them to do as well as other students might, and that in and of itself is not upsetting. Teachers who choose to work with students in urban districts, for example, know that their students are typically not going to do as
well on these tests as students in suburban districts. These students don't have
anywhere near the advantages of wealthier students; they have been disadvantaged in this fashion since birth; and they return to their disadvantaged
existence each day when school is over. It would be foolish to think that these
problems can all be solved by the schools. Yet, each year when the test results
are published by the newspapers, these often incredibly hard-working teachers are castigated by the press and their schools are labeled "dismal failures."
We fully understand teachers who are not fond of standardized tests. The test
is the vehicle for pointing out the differences between the rich and the poor in
terms of school achievement. The politicians and the press, not wanting to
say, "Gee, we have incredibly complex social problems in this country that really need a lot of time, thought, effort, and probably money to fix, and I don't
have a clue as to how to go about solving these problems," instead say, "These
schools are failing our children."

    As a consequence of this situation, some educators become fixed on one
goal and one goal only: improve the test scores. The surest way to improve test
scores is to teach the students how to answer the questions on the test.
(Actually, that isn't the absolute surest way to improve test scores, but without
blatant and direct cheating, it is the best way.) As we mentioned earlier, if the
test were the exact same thing as the instructional goal, this really wouldn't be
a problem. However, standardized tests have certain restrictions that don't
exist for classroom testing. Four of these restrictions are

1. The assumption of a common curriculum among students

2. A testing format that can be given under standard conditions

3. A response format that can be graded relatively economically

4. A fairly limited amount of testing time available

Thus, the type of complex, engaging, longer-term, project-related assessment involving interactions with peers and manipulative materials geared to issues in the local town is pretty much out of the question.

Approximations and compromises have to be made in the development of standardized measures. What can be done in a reasonable amount of time? What instructional goals can we assume have been covered by all students who will be taking this measure? What can be scored objectively without an inordinate cost? How can a lot of material be covered on the assessment in a fairly short amount of time? The answers to each of these questions pushes the assessment developer farther and farther away from the kinds of assessments you like to have in your classroom and closer to a multiple choice format assessing somewhat generic skills. For example, it is particularly hard in science and social studies to come up with a curriculum that is common across school districts, as districts like to develop their own ideas along these lines. And when the state develops a standardized measure, the measure pretty much defines the instructional goals in these areas.

At best, a standardized measure can only cover some of the learning goals we are interested in and can only do so in a limited number of formats. It takes up too much time to change the item format too many times on a test. Thus, even a well-thought-out and professionally constructed standardized measure can only cover a portion of the instructional goals and is somewhat limited in format. Let's start there. Take a test that covers certain aspects of the instructional goals for a grade level and does so with a limited number of item formats. Add to that strong pressure on teachers to have their students perform well on the assessments. Now let's look at some possible approaches to preparing students to take this test.

Test Preparation Approaches

1. Teach your students as well as you possibly can without paying attention to the standardized test and hope that the students' abilities will show through on the assessment.

2. Spend most of your time in instruction as you normally do, but spend some time going over the item formats to be found on the assessment so that your students will be familiar with these formats and will not suffer on the assessment due to lack of familiarity.

(continued)

3. Analyze the content of the assessment, make certain you cover that content in your regular instructional program, then work on item format and test-taking skills as well.

4. Analyze the content of the assessment and restructure your instructional program around that content exclusively. Then, in addition, engage in Item 3 above.

5. Teach students directly how to answer questions that are similar to the questions on the assessment.

6. Teach students directly to answer the questions on the assessment.

7. Provide students with the answers on the assessment.

What you may find surprising here is that short of Approach 7, each of the other choices has proponents. Not only that, there are people who argue that unless you are doing some of these things you are denying your students the opportunity to do their best on the assessment. Actually, you may find yourself in agreement with some of these positions. Let's see if we can make a reasonable claim for every position with the exception of Approach 7.

Approach 1 is not too difficult to defend. If the teacher is confident that the assessment is clearly and directly related to the instructional goals that the instruction is based on, and if the item format is close to the instructional format (what we would consider to be natural) then simply working on one's instructional goals is a perfectly reasonable way to prepare students for the assessment.

Approach 2 is fairly straightforward as well. We might find this situation where we are certain the assessment fits our instructional goals (maybe a committee from the district chose this measure because of its close fit), but we want to make sure the students are comfortable with the item format. We take some instructional time to familiarize them with the format. This gives us more confidence that the information we receive from the assessment results is really telling us about our students' learning and is not reflective of an inability to work well in the format of the test.

Approach 3 is defensible in settings such as a state-mandated testing program. If the state says that certain areas are important enough to be on the test, then we should make sure that they are in our instructional program as well. Additionally, we want to make certain that our students are familiar with the item format for the same reasons as given in Approach 2 above. And finally, we might want to work some with our students on test-taking skills to make certain they are using their talents to the fullest. For example, we might want to review using time wisely since the test will be timed. We also want students to be either guessing or not guessing in the appropriate fashion for the test. Some students seem to come by test-taking skills naturally, and since they are not an intended part of the assessment, it would be best to try to make all students roughly equal in this regard.

Approach 4 is appropriate if the assessment measures all aspects of our instructional goals (determined locally or by the state), either fully or by sampling these aspects on a rotating basis from one year to the next. What we are saying here is that the assessment may be intended to be a complete sample of the intended instructional goals. In that case, if the instruction matches the assessment, it matches the goals as well. Then we would want to engage in the additional Approach 3 activities as explained above.

We know—you're wondering, "How are they going to come up with a rational for Approach 5?" No problem (we wouldn't have put it in there if we couldn't do it). Imagine you are in charge of developing an SAT training program for your school. You know that some of your wealthier students use the professional courses and your school system feels it's only fair for everyone to have the same opportunities. What is your instructional program going to look like? For a large part of it, you are going to be showing students how to answer questions that look like SAT questions. In fact, the best practice is on old SATs, which you can buy from The College Board, who publishes the test.

OK, we kind of snuck Approach 5 in there with a bit of a twist on the idea of what constituted an instructional program. But what about Approach 6? How are we going to justify teaching students the direct items, or tasks that will be on the assessment? Well, think about it for a minute and see if you can come up with an example. Go ahead. Done? All right, here is what we came up with. You are training pianists for the Van Cliburn competition. We can just see you smacking your forehead and saying, "Why didn't I think of that?" For the Van Cliburn competition, students work on exactly what they are going to play in the competition. At some levels, we can compare this to school. Band and choral competitions, the football team, the drama club, and even the yearbook staff all work directly on that which is to be the assessment.

Approach 7? Well, Approach 7 really looks like cheating in almost all settings with the possible exception of the driver's license test. We think some states provide a long list of questions and answers, then just sample some of those questions for the test. Besides, just the thought of the Department of Motor Vehicles can generate thoughts that none of us would like made public.

What Should the Goal of Student Preparation Be?

Obviously not all of the approaches listed above are appropriate in all settings. We would hope that most of the time the decision would have to be made among the top three approaches with regard to a standardized assessment. But what is a reasonable goal for student preparation that both is fair to the student and provides useful information about the student? Our notion is that preparation should let the student's real abilities show through. There should be enough preparation that the student isn't confused by the format, doesn't run out of time before getting a chance to work on each item or task, knows how to bring his or her abilities to bear on an item or a task, and generally leaves the assessment believing that the results of the assessment will be an accurate reflection of his or her ability or knowledge. Another way to put this is, "No surprises."

If you are working with students who are going to take an end-of-year standardized assessment such as the Iowa Test of Basic Skills (ITBS), the first thing you have to ask yourself (either as an individual teacher or as a school district) is, "How will I interpret the results?" Assume for argument's sake that the ITBS represented the best match of test to instructional goals and sequencing in your district, but that this match was not perfect. If you do not care that your students will not do well on some areas that are not covered in your instructional program by the time the test is administered (or, in the area of math, that you haven't covered this material recently), then you can use Approach 2 or even Approach 1 if you feel your students will not have a problem with the test format. In interpreting the results, you will need to concentrate on those areas that you have covered. This approach may not be practical. A skeptical public may not be placated by a statement that they "shouldn't worry about low percentiles because we didn't cover some of the material that was on the test."

Another approach to interpreting the ITBS would be to say, "The ITBS pretty much measures what we are interested in, so let's make sure all of the material is covered in our curriculum before we give the test. That way, we can make relatively straightforward interpretations of the results." If this is your approach, then you definitely want to take at least Approach 3 and maybe Approach 4.

We aren't going to pursue the preparation approaches to standardized assessments any further. It is now up to you to carefully consider the uses of the assessment and interpretations to be made from it and make your preparation choices according to your considerations.

What Is the Best Way to Get Students Ready for a Test?

This is a pretty broad topic, but we can give a few suggestions that might be helpful. First, the goal should simply be "No surprises." If a student does not do well on the assessment, it should be because the student does not have the requisite skills being assessed. Students should be familiar with the types of activities they will be asked to do on the assessment. They should understand time limits and how their performance will be scored, and they should have some idea of their abilities relative to the assessment. This last piece of information is useful because students need to have an idea of how well they are doing as they move through the assessment. Without any sense of how hard the assessment is relative to their ability, they might develop anxiety if they think they are not doing well or indifference if they feel the tasks are too simple.

It has been our experience in working with students that the more help they need, the more direct and more closely tied to the assessment the instruction has to be. Weaker students have trouble applying generic instructions to specific assessments. If the assessment involves novel tasks or tasks in which the students do not have a lot of experience, it is often useful to show students what a strong and a weak performance look like. For example, if students are going to be asked to write an essay about a personal topic, it can be very helpful to show them what strong essays and weak essays look like. What will be important in the grading? Should students focus on content or on good sentence structure and form? If students do not know what they will be graded on, it will be difficult for them to show what they can do.

How Do Classroom Assessments Relate to Standardized Assessments?

Classroom assessments and preparing students for them are a whole different ball game from standardized assessments. For classroom assessments, we need to turn the system around. Here we need to make sure that the assessment fits the instruction, not that the instruction fits the assessment. That is why we argue that the assessment should evolve from the instruction. This ensures that the relationship between the two will be as strong as possible. When the relationship is strong, then regular classroom instruction is preparation for the assessment. All that we need to do is carefully consider the assessment to make certain there are no aspects of the assessment that can cause confusion or lack of validity in the scores. The questions you need to ask here are, "If a student does not do well on this assessment, can I conclude it is because the student didn't have the skills we are working on?" and "If the student does do well, can I conclude the student does have the skills?" Part of the issue is whether the assessment is a good reflection of the instructional goals, but it is also important to make sure that students are ready to take the assessment. Do they understand what is expected of them and what they need to do to demonstrate their ability?

How Can I Get Students to Really Work on the Topics That Are Important and Not Study Material That Is Less Important?

We are so glad you asked. We have a real simple answer here, one that we have alluded to before. If you want students to do something, tell them what you want them to do. On projects and performances, be explicit about what you want. On essays, make your prompts communicate clearly what the expectations are. On tests, make a test blueprint to help you develop the test, and give the test blueprint to the students in advance so that they can study from it. Test blueprint? Yep. This is one of the best ideas we have in this book. Here's the idea.

Let's say you have been working on a unit on probability and statistics in a 10th-grade math course (don't panic, we're professionals in this area). There's been a bit of tough sledding in this unit and you would like the students to give it one more thorough review before moving on to the next unit. You want them to focus on the important concepts that they might be able to take with them in later years. So here's what you do. Sit down with the unit and go through everything that you have worked on in class. Toss the material that isn't important and get down to the ideas that you really want student to comprehend. Now make an outline of these topics and ideas. The level of detail is up to you, but we can typically manage this in one page. Now that you have the outline, prioritize the topics by putting point values on the assessment next to each topic. We always like our assessments to be based on 100 points, but you do whatever makes you comfortable. Your final outline might look something like the following:

Test Blueprint for Statistics and Probability Unit

    I. Central tendency (30 points)
       A. Means (10 points)
       B. Medians (10 points)
       C. Modes (10 points)
   II. Variability (20 points)
       A. Range (5 points)
       B. Variance (10 points)
       C. Standard deviation (5 points)
  III. Probability (20 points)
       A. Sample spaces (10 points)
       B. Additive rule (5 points)
       C. Multiplicative rule (5 points)
  IV. Calculating probabilities (30 points)
       A. Independent events (15 points)
       B. Joint occurrences (15 points)

This test blueprint now serves three functions. First, we can examine it to see if it really represents what we want students to study. Does it truly reflect what we believe to be important? Second, it serves as a guide to writing the assessment. We can make sure that the point distribution on the assessment is reflective of our goals. Third, we can give the blueprint to the students well in advance of the assessment to serve as a study guide. This lets students know exactly what we think they should be studying. It absolutely eliminates "You didn't tell us what would be on the test," "I studied all sorts of material you didn't test us on," "I didn't know that would be on the test," and other similar complaints. The folks we know who have adopted this idea truly seem to like it. Give it a try.

To sum up this chapter, we have been looking at the issue of preparing students for assessments. A lot of what we have focused on concerns standardized assessments, since they are such an important part of classroom life today. We examined a variety of approaches for preparing students for standardized assessments and the justifications for those approaches. The underlying principle here is that unless students are ready to take an assessment, we are likely to misinterpret the results. Our rule of thumb for getting students ready is "no surprises."

CHAPTER 10

Scoring and Communicating Results

In this chapter, we are going to look at what happens when the assessment is over. How do we score and communicate results to students? Actually, saying the assessment is over is not really correct; although the process of gathering the information is over, much of the important work in the assessment process still lies ahead. You have to evaluate the work that the students have done and communicate your impressions back to the students. For objective assessments such as short answer and multiple choice, this isn't too difficult (although grades typically have to be assigned to the assessments, which poses another set of issues).

What Are Some General Rules for Scoring and Grading?

To begin, let's be clear that we are talking about scoring and grading right now. We will talk about other forms of feedback a little later. The first rule for scoring and grading is to get your system organized before you give the assessment to the students. You should have a good sense of what you are going to do before you get started. We typically like to use a scoring system based on a total of 100 points. This simplifies combining information down the road. For many types of assessments, however, you will be using letter grades, or perhaps even a check/check-minus/check-plus sort of a system. These are fine, too; you just have to think about how you are going to combine all of the information you have into an overall plan for coming up with grades and providing feedback to students. If you have a bunch of letter grades, another bunch of number grades, and a third bunch of checks and check pluses, what are you going to do when it comes time to summarize performance? It's important to think about this in advance.

The second rule of scoring and grading is fairness. It is absolutely critical that you treat all of your students fairly in your assessment activities. Students are keenly aware of any hint of playing favorites. Sometimes they find favoritism when it isn't even there. Your system must not only be fair, it must also look fair. To this end, you need to make sure that when you grade an assessment activity, you do so without knowing whose it is (to the extent possible). You determine the grade based only on the performance or product you have in front of you, not on the student. Once you have evaluated the assessment, you can think about what it means for the student in terms of future instruction; you shouldn't be doing that while you are evaluating the assessment. *This is an important point.* As a teacher and an advocate of the student, you are naturally going to want to take the results of an assessment and put them to use in the best interest of the student. But first, you must make a fair and objective evaluation of the assessment activity.

The third rule is to reflect on the information you have at hand. We sometimes have a tendency to jump to conclusions about assessment. For example, what does almost all the students doing poorly on a task mean? Maybe the students weren't working hard on this task. Maybe they simply weren't engaged. Maybe the task wasn't taught very well. If almost all students did poorly, there is clearly some sort of general problem. Maybe the task wasn't presented very well. Go back and look at what you asked students to do. Were you clear in your directions? Was there a potential for misinterpreting the results? One of the most basic ideas we can communicate to you in working with students and assessments is that *the information has to make sense.* If the data you have at hand don't make sense to you, don't trust them. We once got a call from a school principal who was concerned that a sixth-grade girl who had always done well on her standardized test scores had failed miserably on the reading portion of the most recent testing. She had done as well as usual on all other components of the test. The principal was distrustful of the results and wanted a second opinion. It seemed suspicious to us as well. Without going into too much detail, the problem turned out to be that the girl had gone home sick halfway through the reading test and the teacher had forgotten to pull her answer sheet from the pile of turned-in student tests.

The fourth rule (and this is our rule; some people disagree with it) is to give credit where credit is due. We strongly believe in partial credit where partial knowledge or ability is shown. When a student gets a wrong answer on a math problem, particularly a complex math problem, we believe in looking at that problem to see how close the student got to the right answer. Look at this example.

Juanita plays on her school basketball team. She has averaged 12 points per game for the first four basketball games this season. How many points must she score during the next game to increase her average to 14 points per game?

$$12 \qquad \overset{2}{1}4 \qquad 70$$
$$\underline{\times 4} \qquad \underline{\times 5} \qquad \underline{-48}$$
$$48 \qquad 70 \qquad 22$$

answer ___20___

Figure 10.1.

This is a bit of an extreme case, but what appears to have happened is that the student miscopied the answer from her work. Now we don't want to reward being sloppy in copying answers, but we are assessing mathematics here. If this were a 10-point problem, we would probably give about 8 points for it. Losing 2 points out of 10 for a silly mistake ought to be enough of a reminder to students to be neat. Getting no points at all would obviously make the point even more strongly, but we feel that would be punitive and not productive. Now look at another student's working of the same problem.

Juanita plays on her school basketball team. She has averaged 12 points per game for the first four basketball games this season. How many points must she score during the next game to increase her average to 14 points per game?

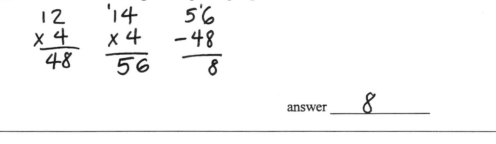

$$12 \qquad \overset{1}{1}4 \qquad 5\overset{\cdot}{6}$$
$$\underline{\times 4} \qquad \underline{\times 4} \qquad \underline{-48}$$
$$48 \qquad 56 \qquad 8$$

answer ___8___

Figure 10.2.

This is a student who has many of the ideas necessary for solving the problem but hasn't yet put all the steps together for a correct answer. We would award about 6 points out of 10 for this work.

Those are some general rules for looking at what we are doing. Now let's turn to some specifics.

What Are Rubrics, and How Are They Developed?

Five years ago nobody knew what the word rubric meant. Now rubrics are falling out of our desk drawers. So what is a rubric? Fundamentally, it is a written description of how some assessment is going to be scored. A useful reference on rubrics is Goodrich (1996). Rubrics are used for all types of assessments, and they come in a variety of formats. Let's look at a rubric that might be developed for the math problem in Figures 10.1 and 10.2.

Holistic Scoring Rubric for Mathematics

Level 1: The student's response shows a full command and solid understanding of the mathematics related to this task. (9 to 10 points)

Level 2: The student's response shows that the student comprehends most of the mathematics in the task, but there is an area or areas of weakness. (6 to 8 points)

Level 3: The student's response shows that there is progress on the mathematics related to the task, but there are substantial areas of weakness. (4 to 7 points)

Level 4: The student's response indicates little or no progress toward comprehension of the mathematics related to this task. (0 to 3 points)

What does the rubric let us do? It gives us some notion of how we want to look at this and other problems in terms of grading. This rubric is holistic in nature. It instructs us to look at the response as a whole and make a general assessment of it. This rubric could be used for almost any type of mathematics item at almost any level. The other general form of rubric is called analytical. It specifies components of an assessment and awards points to the successful completion of the components. Many people believe that analytical scoring provides more comprehensive instructions on how to score and therefore produces scores that are more reliable across different scorers. Others prefer the more general nature of holistic rubrics and are willing to sacrifice some reliability in exchange for the generality. Here is an analytical rubric for the problem in Figures 10.1 and 10.2.

Analytical Rubric for Mathematics Problem

Problem Setup: The student has properly interpreted what is to be done in the problem and has an effective system set up for working the problem (up to 5 points for clear evidence of the problem being set up in an appropriate fashion).

Problem Organization: The student has organized the steps of the problem properly and has worked through the steps in the right fashion (up to 3 points for showing evidence that the steps of the problem have been organized in a proper fashion).

Execution: The student has carried out the pertinent calculations for answering the problem correctly (a loss of 1 point for each calculation error found in the problem).

Evaluation and Estimation: The student has evaluated the likelihood of his or her answer being correct and appears to have compared it against an estimation of what a reasonable answer might look like (up to 2 points for evidence of successful evaluation of the correct answer).

As can be seen, the analytical rubric provides somewhat more in the way of specific things to look at and grade, but a total of ten points is once again possible. We should note, however, that this is still a bit on the generic side for an analytical rubric. If you want to explore rubrics for mathematics, you might consider *A Collection of Performance Tasks and Rubrics: High School Mathematics* by Danielson and Marquez (1998).

What use might rubrics be to you in the classroom? We think there are a couple of possibilities here. First, they are helpful in grading, particularly if you use a variety of modes of assessment. A holistic rubric in a subject area provides a general guide for looking at student products. Second, they are useful to provide to students to help them think about their work. Third, they are useful when talking to parents about student work. A final note before leaving this topic: you may have noticed that there was no place in either sample rubric for copying the correct answer into the space provided. If you want to grade on that, and if you are providing rubrics to students, put that information in the rubric.

How Are Target Essays Used in Scoring?

Another approach to scoring essays is to use what are called target essays. These are essays on the assigned topic that represent performance that typifies a certain level of expertise. For example, if you wanted to grade an essay on a 6-point scale, and if you used the same or a similar prompt or question for the essay, you could pick essays which were exemplars for each of the six levels. In essence you would be saying, "This is what a '6' essay looks like," or

"This typifies a score of '3' on this assignment." In scoring the essays, you then look at each new essay to see which of the target essays it is closest to. This then becomes the score for that essay.

There is a useful variation to this. Instead of picking essays that typify each of the score levels, you can pick essays that typify the break points between two levels of scoring. In other words, you pick an essay that represents the cut between a "5" and a "6." If the essay you are scoring is better than the target, then it is a "6"; if it is worse than the target, then it is at most a "5." This would be the "5/6" cut essay. You then compare it to the essay that represents the cut between a "4" and a "5," (the 4/5 essay) and so on until you have settled on a final score. This approach has two advantages over the previous approach. First, you only have to have five target essays instead of six. Second, it is usually easier to look at an essay and say, "This is better than the "4/5," but not as good as the "5/6," than it is to say, "This essay is closer to the "5" than it is to the "6."

How Many Points Should an Assessment Be Worth?

Different people use different systems for scoring assessments. Some folks strongly prefer scoring everything on an A, B, C, D, and F scale; others advocate a point system of 100 points; still others develop a score with as many points as the assessment seems to call for (such as the 6-point scale used in the example above). So what is the best system? The ultimate answer is obviously up to you, but let us make a few points on this. What do you need to do with the numbers? If you are teaching at a grade level that requires letter grades for report cards, then you have to combine the scores from the various assessments into the final grade. If you have a combination of number scores, letter grades, and checkmarks, this can become a bit challenging. Also, it becomes harder for students to keep track of their grade if they don't know how all of the different systems are going to be tallied. We recommend trying to work with a system that assigns 100 points to each assignment when possible and that assigns a percentage of the total grade to each assessment activity. If each assessment has a 100-point maximum and has a percentage of the total grade for the marking period associated with it, it is pretty easy to keep track of where you are. Another useful approach is to have a total of 100 points for the marking period. This is often easier to use if you have some assessments that are worth 6 points, others worth 20, others worth 1, and so on.

No matter which system you use, you should start by determining how much each assessment is to be worth in the grand scheme of things. Don't worry about how to score it at the beginning, just determine what proportion of the total grade it should be. Consider this example.

Roughing Out a System for Grading

A Sixth-Grade Social Studies Class

1. Marking period exam (20%)

2. Paper on Marco Polo's exploration (20%)

3. Group project on the development of the Renaissance (20%)

4. Five chapter quizzes (25% @ 5% for each quiz)

5. Contribution to class video project (15%)

6. Bonus points for contributing during regular class time (up to 5% extra credit)

This general guide provides us with what we need to get started on determining how to set up the scoring system. We have the general system in place (and we ought to tell the students about it); now we have to work out the details. Here we might want to work out a system that simply adds up to 100 points total. We could turn each of these assessments into the proportion of the total they are—the paper on Marco Polo would be scored on a 20-point scale, for example. Or we could score each of these activities on a 100-point scale, then multiply the scores by the proportions attributed to them. In either system, we also have to figure out how to work in the bonus points for contributing to the class. In all likelihood, the easiest way to do this is to simply come up with a system for earning each of the points, then just adding them into the total.

How Should Levels of Performance Be Set?

We have looked at how to score essays with rubrics—scoring tests simply requires setting point values for each of the questions then determining how to score the questions. There is one other element to take under consideration, however, and it is frequently overlooked. What should be an A and what should be a B? This gets overlooked because people don't think seriously about the fact that there actually are options here. We tend to think in terms of the following for determining As, Bs, Cs, Ds and Fs:

90-100   A
80-89   B
70-79   C
60-69   D
Below 60 F

We might, of course, put in some room for pluses and minuses, but the basic idea is the same. Here is another system that is used.

93-100   A
85-92   B
77-84   C
70-76   D
Below 70 F

There is an assumption in both of these systems that is fundamentally untenable, but we almost never think about it. The assumption is that the assessments that are written are always of a level of difficulty that makes a 90 or a 93 actually be A work, an 86 be B work, etc. We may usually come close to this, but basically there is no justification for this without a careful examination of the assessment. One test may be particularly difficult, another quite easy, and a third may be very easy for 80% of the grade and very difficult for the last 20%. If you are skeptical, consider this.

Let's say your instructional goal concerns knowledge of the U.S. Constitution and you have been studying the Bill of Rights. You want to know if the students know what rights are guaranteed under the First Amendment. You might ask

1. What rights are guaranteed under the First Amendment?

This is pretty straightforward. It poses the question you are interested in, and the students must provide the answer. Now, basically there are five rights guaranteed under the first amendment: freedom of assembly, freedom of speech, freedom of the press, freedom of religion, and the right to petition the government to redress grievances. A student may only list freedom of speech, the press, and religion and think he or she has it right as the other two typically get less play. Let's change the question slightly, to

1. What five rights are guaranteed under the First Amendment?

This is a change most people would not even notice, but it would make the question easier to get right because it points out how many rights there are. Here is another alternative.

1. There are five rights guaranteed under the First Amendment. Name three of them.

Now the question is easier still. Let's play some more.

1. Four of the rights guaranteed under the First Amendment are freedom of speech, of the press, of religion, and to peaceable assembly. What is the fifth right?

Now the question is quite hard. If you don't know everything, you can't even get partial credit for knowing four of the five rights. Let's turn in the other direction for one final version.

1. Which of the following is not guaranteed under the First Amendment?
    a. Freedom of speech
    b. Right to petition the government to redress grievances
    c. Right to keep and bear arms
    d. Freedom of religion

Now you don't really need to know the First Amendment at all. If you know that C is the Second Amendment, that's all you need to get the answer right. The point of this little exercise is that with the same instructional goal, a question on an assessment can be fairly easy or fairly hard. It depends on how we put the question together. The notion that 90 and above should always be an A seems rather arbitrary at best. Yet you may be required by your school district to make 90 and above an A. So what are you going to do? Well, we have a suggestion.

Once you have written an assessment, we recommend you engage in a little thought exercise. Imagine what might be called the Minimal A student, the student whose performance on the assessment represents the lowest A you want to give. Lower performance is clearly a B, but this performance squeaks in with an A. Now look at the first question on the assessment. How would the Minimal A student perform on this question? You might say, "To deserve an A, you have to know this answer completely." If the question is worth 6 points, you write a 6 down next to it as the Minimal A level of performance. Now go to question 2. Let's say this one is worth 8 points and you think, "Well, the minimal A student has to know these aspects of this question, but he or she could lose one point on this aspect and still be doing A work, so the Minimal A student has to get a 7 on this question." You put a 7 down next to that question. You continue on until you have completed the test, marking down what the

Minimal A student did each time. Then you add up the scores and come up with the cut score for the Minimal A student. It might be 94 or 86, but whatever you come up with, it is what you have determined it should be.

Once this is done, you need to go back through the test one more time, this time bearing in mind the Minimal Pass student. This is the lowest performance you will still give a passing grade to. You engage in the same process and generate a total score that represents the cut between passing and failing. Now you are tired of taking the test, so you just divvy up the difference between the A/B and the D/F cuts into equal intervals. For example, if the A/B cut is 88 and the D/F cut is 64, then you would lay out the final grade cuts like this.

88-100	A
80-88	B
72-79	C
64-71	D
63 and below	F

These cuts take into account how difficult you feel the questions on the assessment are. They allow you to make adjustments on the various cut scores based on your assessment of the question difficulties. Now there is one other possibility to consider here. You may say, "But my district mandates that all tests be on the '90 and above is an A' system. Now what do I do?" Fairly easy—adjust a few test questions to get your assessment closer to the 90 and above requirement. On this test, we would make two or three questions a little bit easier to answer. This will bring up all of the levels a few points and get you pretty close to where you want to be. This isn't rocket science, so pretty close ought to be good enough.

What Should Go on a Paper, and What Else Should I Do to Communicate Results?

This is an area of assessment that still does not get a lot of attention, even with the revolution in the area of assessment. We tend to think of the score or grade that summarizes performance as the only communication that matters. The commentary that accompanies a total score or a letter grade can mean a lot to a student. We have touched on this topic, but it's worth a quick revisit here. Our concern is that the commentary on a paper or test be related to the paper or test and not involve judgments about the student in general. On a test that involves short answer or essay, it is very helpful to give students an idea of why they lost points when they did lose points. If it is a paper or a report that is being scored, explain why it was a C and not a B and what the student can do to get a better mark the next time. On an extended writing task that has to be revised and turned in again, be sure you don't become an editor for the paper, taking ownership away from the student. If an area needs to be developed more, say that it needs more development, but don't do the development.

In this chapter, we've looked at what happens after the assessment has been handed in. In some respects the student is done, but you have a lot of work remaining. This is important work in the instructional process. You need to keep in mind that you are evaluating the work that the student has done. At the same time that you always have an eye on the instructional consequences of the evaluation a student receives, you should not let the instructional part of your job interfere with the evaluation of the assessment. Students need to know honestly how they are doing. Once this has been determined, then you can return to your advocacy role to help them do better next time. It is not helpful to give students false information about how well they are doing in order to keep them from being discouraged. They need honest feedback and then help and encouragement from you as their teacher.

CHAPTER 11

Planning Parent-
Teacher Conferences

One of the most important aspects of assessment is the communication of assessment results to the various constituencies who need them. Among these constituencies are parents. Your humble author team has an awful lot of years in as parents of kindergarteners through 12th-graders, and we can promise you that parent-teacher communication is one of the weakest links in the chain of educational progress. The weakness works both ways and varies substantially from district to district, teacher to teacher, and parent to parent. There is a lot of room for improvement on all fronts, but the front we are talking to here is teachers, so what follows is our perspective on communicating to parents.

A story might be useful in setting a context for this chapter. It has to do with the birth of the first author's son, Ben. About two hours after Ben was born, a nurse asked if we wanted a circumcision performed. (A point here if there are any nurses reading this: Ask the mother, not the father. The whole idea of this brings back long-suppressed trauma in men.) I told the nurse we did want a circumcision. The nurse said that a parental release form needed to be signed, and my first thought was, "That's ridiculous, my parents live in Florida." This is related to parent-teacher conferences, you're wondering? The point is that parenting is often a fairly new phenomenon for many parents. Parents don't usually come to you with decades of experience and wisdom in parenting—some have a lot, some have only a little. They might be new to dealing with an adolescent. But even if you are equally new to teaching, they are coming to you as a professional who is concerned about their child. You don't have to have all the answers, but don't expect them to, either. Parents come in all shapes, sizes, backgrounds, and dispositions. You need to be open and flexible and have a good command of the information you want to present and discuss concerning their child.

The most common form of communicating is the parent-teacher conference; that will be the focus of this chapter. We will also look at other vehicles for communicating to parents, but we'll concentrate on the parent-teacher conference.

Why Are Parent-Teacher Conferences Important?

A word to our readers who are preservice student teachers or teachers without a lot of experience: Parent-teacher conferences are important. They are important in their own right in that they provide an opportunity to get together with the other critical educators in the lives of your students, their parents. They are also important because the parents you are talking with represent the community in which you work. If you do parent-teacher conferences poorly, it reflects on you as a teacher. That may be unfair, but it is certainly true.

The parent-teacher conference is an opportunity for you to learn about your students and to enlist their parents more directly in the education of their children. It lets you build a team to help your students achieve their goals. Many teachers look on parent-teacher conferences as a nuisance, or even something to be dreaded, but they are really an opportunity to build on the work that you are doing with your students. We think it is important to approach them as the opportunity that they can be. Let's take a look at several examples of parent-teacher interchanges that we can use for discussion purposes.

Parent-Teacher Conference with Mr. and Mrs. Jankowski

Billy Jankowski is a fifth-grade student in Teacher Collins's class. He is an average student whose strengths are in mathematics and science, but who has trouble in reading, particularly with getting any of the subtleties in text. He gets his homework in on time, and it is usually very well done, but he contributes very little to class discussions and activities. He dislikes writing and has very poor handwriting. He only has one friend in class and is rather withdrawn. The parent-teacher conference is taking place in late October.

Teacher C: Are you the Jankowskis?

Mr. J: Yes.

Teacher C: Please have a seat.

Mrs. J: Thank you.

Teacher C: Well, let's see, you're Billy's parents. Let me just turn to my material on Billy. Oh, yes. Well, Billy is doing fairly well in math and science, but his literacy skills are rather weak. Did you know he has trouble with his handwriting? It's quite hard to read.

Mrs. J: No.

Teacher C: Well, that's probably not the biggest concern I have with Billy. He really needs to get going on the development of his reading skills. He is lagging pretty far behind the other students on this. He doesn't have many friends in class. Does he have a lot of brothers and sisters?

Mrs. J: He's an only child.

Teacher C: Well, do you have any questions about Billy?

Mrs. J: I guess not.

Teacher C: Well, it's been nice to meet you.

Parent-Teacher Conference with Mrs. Marsten

Tory Jackson is a sixth-grade student in Teacher Thompson's class. She lives with her mom, Sarah Marsten, and her stepfather. Tory is a high-energy student who does fairly well in most subject areas but tends to be a little flighty and forgetful. She enjoys writing and is a strong writer. She is also very artistically inclined. Her mathematics work would be stronger if she paid a little bit more attention to detail. She is one of the more popular students in the class.

Teacher T: Hi, are you Tory's mom?

Mrs. M: Yes, I am. You're Teacher T?

Teacher T: Yes, please come in and have a seat. It's nice to meet you.

Mrs. M: Thank you, it's good to meet you, too.

Teacher T: It's great to have Tory in class. She brings such energy to everything that she does. I have Tory's work to date recorded in my grade book here, and I've pulled out some of Tory's more recent work in case you would like to look at it. Let me start, though, by asking you what questions you have or if there are any topics you would particularly like to go over tonight.

Mrs. M: Thank you. I think we are just generally interested in how well Tory is doing and what we might do to help.

Teacher T: That's great. Let me begin with a brief overview, then we'll move toward some specifics. I want to be sure to cover what seem to be Tory's strengths and weaknesses as well. Once we've done that, let's talk about what we can do together to make this the best year possible for Tory.

That should be enough of an introduction to two rather different settings to begin the discussion. If you were a parent, which teacher would you prefer for your son or daughter? Let's look at the first conference with Teacher Collins and the Jankowskis. Here we tried to put in almost every mistake you could make in a parent-teacher conference. Look back at the interchange and see how many mistakes you can find. Go ahead, we'll wait.

Here's the list we came up with:

1. There is no greeting here. This classroom is like your home, especially as far as guests coming into it are concerned.

2. These may be Billy's parents, but they may not be the Jankowskis. They may be Billy's Mom and her husband who is Billy's stepfather. Better to start off with "Are you Billy's parents (folks)?" or even "Hi, I'm Teacher Collins, are you here for Billy?" "Are you the Jankowskis?" sounds like an interrogation. The best thing is to find out who is coming and what relation they are to Billy. One of the authors once had an older sister come in for a student, who was mistaken for the student's mother.

3. The first statement about Billy is negative. Please, *please, **please*** start parent-teacher conferences with a positive statement about the student.

4. Teacher Collins is not ready to receive Mr. and Mrs. Jankowski. She doesn't have the material ready for them.

5. The first piece of information is included in a barrage of information. There are a number of really important points here. They get lost in this fusillade of information that ends on a criticism of Billy's handwriting.

6. There is no follow-up or encouragement to the parents to contribute to the conversation.

7. The second bunch of information has the same problem as the first. Too much information all at once.

8. Getting this meeting over seems to be Teacher Collins' primary objective. She certainly has accomplished it, but what has she gained?

Let's contrast this first parent-teacher conference with the second one. Here Teacher Thompson begins the conversation by addressing Mrs. Marsten as "Tory's mom." That's who Mrs. Marsten is for purposes of this meeting, Tory's mom. Next, she welcomes Mrs. Marsten to her classroom and immediately says something positive about Tory. She also lets Mrs. Marsten know that she is prepared for the meeting. Mrs. Marsten has already received a number of signals from Teacher Thompson. She is welcome; Teacher Thompson is organized; Teacher Thompson likes her child. This is a meeting that is going to go well. The next thing that Teacher Thompson does is let Mrs. Marsten know that this is her meeting as well as Teacher Thompson's. She wants to know what Tory's mom's concerns are. We leave the conversation with Teacher Thompson pointing out that they will be discussing weaknesses as well as strengths and working toward what they can do together to help Tory.

We've seen how to do it and how not to do it. Let's work from these examples to some goals and general principles for communicating with parents.

What Is the Goal of a Parent-Teacher Conference?

Specific goals for conferences concerning specific students will naturally vary somewhat from student to student, but consider the following as general goals for parent-teacher conferences.

Your overall goal is straightforward. You want to let the student's parents know how the student is doing. You want to get to know the parents a little and see how you can work with the parents to help the student. At a little bit more specific level, you'd like to know what goals and aspirations the student's parents have for the student; whether they are willing to participate in the student's education at home; and whether their perception of their child coincides with your perception. Frequently, what you think about a student and what his or her parents think about the student may be substantially at odds. Keep two things in mind about this. First, many students actually behave quite differently in school and at home. (We are the parents of some of those children.) Second, you have broad experience with lots and lots of different children; the parents only really know their children and their children's friends. Their normative group is much smaller, and these are their children. Joseph Zelnick, a colleague and a wonderful trainer of reading specialists, put the situation beautifully in this eloquent but simple quote.

> Remember, these are the very best children these parents have.

A student who is the bane of your existence is still the apple of his mother's eye. Parents often come to parent-teacher conferences with a true sense of trepidation. They are going to hear an evaluation of the most important thing in their lives. Let's look at some ideas that can make these interactions be as productive as they can be.

What Should Be Included, What Should Be Avoided?

We have a short list of dos and don'ts that should make parent-teacher conferences go better. We hope you find them useful.

Pointers for Parent-Teacher Conferences

1. Of all the information in this chapter, this is the most important: Your first and primary goal in a parent-teacher conference is to convince the parents that you are sincerely concerned about their child. If you can communicate to parents that you are on their child's side, you can tell them almost anything about the student. If, on the other hand, parents are led to believe that you don't like or are indifferent about their child, you have set yourself up with a pair of opponents, maybe even enemies. We used to say that you should convince parents that you like their child, but on occasion this may be hard to do convincingly. It's not necessary for you to like all of your students, but it really is your responsibility to be in their corner. If you're not, you might want to think about selling life insurance as an alternative career.

2. Welcome the parents into your classroom. This is common courtesy.

3. Be sure that the first thing you say about the student is positive. Parents aren't really ready to hear anything negative about their child until some level of rapport has been reached.

4. Be prepared. Have your materials organized. If at all possible, have some of the student's material available to show parents. In particular, if you have specific points you want to make concerning the student's work, have examples to show the parents to make the point clear.

5. Focus on behavior and facts. Try not to make broad generalizations about the student. It is better to say something like "Harold and I are working on developing a broader range of sentence structure. Here is one of his early papers. You can see he pretty much relied on simple declarative sentences. Here on his most recent submission, you can see that he is beginning to branch out a little" than to say "Harold is very limited in his approach to writing. I've been trying to help him grow in this area."

6. Ask the parents what their concerns are. You may learn things that are important for you in terms of working with the student.

7. Explore the potential of having the parents contribute more actively in the academic growth of their child. Some parents are eager to work with their children, others are not so eager, others are not able.

8. Don't make promises you can't keep. Remember you have a whole class of children to work with, sometimes several classes. Don't overcommit to one set of parents to the detriment of the others.

Before leaving this topic, it is important to emphasize that different situations will require different approaches—but this list should be useful in most situations.

How Do I Handle Really Difficult Cases?

Sometimes you have to talk to parents about particularly troubling cases. These often involve behavioral or emotional problems, not academic ones, but let's spend a few lines on the topic anyway. If you have a situation with a child that you feel requires you to have to communicate truly bad news to a parent, or if the student is causing severe problems in your classroom, you need to plan carefully for how you are going to approach the situation. First of all, we recommend talking to your principal about the situation. Even if your principal isn't an interpersonal rocket scientist, you have nonetheless informed him or her of the situation and asked for assistance. As a second step, talk to one or more of your colleagues, especially a colleague who has a reputation for being good at handling difficult situations. Third, practice what you are going to do. You may even want to role-play with a colleague. Fourth, be sure you have your facts in order and stick to the facts. Fifth, be as honest and straightforward as you can be. And finally, approach the problem with the student's best interests at heart.

If you are talking to the parents of the class bully or of a student who is severely withdrawn or whose academic performance has severely declined in recent weeks, try to consider the nature of the problem from the student's perspective. Also try to think about the parents' perspective. Just as no one wants to have their child be picked on, no one wants to be the parents of the class bully. Use the supports that exist within your district to help you out. You cannot solve every problem in your class, and you may not be the best person to solve certain problems. You are part of a team in your school; let your colleagues do their jobs as you do yours.

What About Parents Who Don't Show?

This is one of the toughest problems facing educators. If you can't get the parents into your class to talk about their child, what are you to do? Parents don't show for a variety of reasons. Some work during the times you would normally meet with parents. Can you extend or modify your schedule? Some single parents have small children at home and cannot get babysitting help. Can such help be found, or can you meet with a mother who has a 2-year-old in tow? Some parents do not feel welcome in the school. School might not have been the best place for them when they were younger, or it may have been the site of unpleasant prior encounters with school authorities. Can you break through those negative feelings? Maybe a personal letter home would encourage parents to come and talk. Perhaps an initial conference can be done by telephone instead of in person. A colleague of ours told us about having parent conferences include a potluck dinner and an invitation to everyone in the family to come if necessary. She wanted to be certain parents knew how important she felt the conferences were. (If this doesn't sound like your school district, we should mention that this happened in a parochial school in Ireland—but the point is still valid: Sometimes you do have to go out of your way.)

When and How Should I Send a Special Communication Home?

Sometimes the need arises to communicate with parents outside the parent-teacher conference. Sometimes it is necessary to call parents about a specific issue. As parents, we have found that teachers are fairly reluctant to contact parents. Our advice here is simple: If you feel that it would be useful to get in touch with parents about something, go ahead and do it. We are almost always in favor of more communication over less. Send a letter home with a student; send a newsletter home to all students; call a parent if you feel the need. Far more often than not, parents will be glad you did.

In this chapter, we discussed an important and often overlooked aspect of assessment, parent-teacher conferences. The fundamental argument here is to look at parent-teacher conferences as your opportunity to enlist parents in your efforts to reach your instructional goals for your students. Focus on informing parents, using the objective data you have, and concentrate on what you can do to best work with and for the student.

CHAPTER 12

Assessing Students With Special Needs

This chapter looks at issues related to students with special needs. Like the field of assessment, special education has undergone fairly dramatic changes in recent years. One of the most important of these changes concerns the issue of inclusion, of placing students with special challenges into regular classrooms with the assistance of additional help in the classroom. As a regular classroom teacher, you might have a variety of classified students in your classroom. There are a number of instructional issues you need to address in working with these students, one of which has to do with the assessment of those students. It is the assessment of classified and included students that we want to talk about in this chapter.

How Can Students With Special Needs Be Assessed With the Rest of the Class?

Most students who are classified have some level of difficulty in achieving at the same level as the rest of the class in at least some academic areas. The problem for you as a regular classroom teacher is how to assess these students along with the rest of your students. This is a particularly difficult problem, and there really are no simple answers. It is important, however, to start this discussion by noting that there are federal requirements in this area. We'll touch on them here, but if you are teaching classified students, it is important that you are in contact with the Individualized Education Program (IEP) team for your student. These are the people who are charged with the responsibility for developing the instructional objectives for this student. You can look at the federal regulations relating to classified students on the Internet. The best way to find them is to search under "Individuals with Disabilities Education Act."

This act requires (among many other things) that

the Individualized Education Program for each child with a disability include: A statement of the measurable annual goals related to meeting the child's needs that result from the child's disability to enable the child to be involved in and progress in the general curriculum.

In our approach to this question, we try to remain consistent with what we have been saying throughout the book. Assessment flows from instructional goals. The question of assessment for included classified students is really a question of instructional goals for these students. If the instructional goals are the same, the assessment ought to be the same. If the instructional goals are not the same, then the assessments will not be the same. You will not set instructional goals for these students by yourself. In all likelihood, you will work with an IEP team in setting the instructional goals. As might be suggested by the very concept of an IEP, classified students are students whose individual needs must be considered carefully in assessment. Individualization within the context of the classroom is the key here. In all likelihood, the instructional goals for classified students will be constructed to try to be as similar as possible to the regular classroom goals, but there are also likely to be important differences.

In many states classified students are now required to take the state's standardized testing program. This fairly recent change in requirements for classified students has substantial consequence for classroom teachers. If this is the situation you are in, then you must do your best to make sure your classified students are as ready as possible to take these tests, but at the same time you also need to respect the requirements of the students' IEP. In most situations, you will find that classified students will be permitted certain accommodations according to their IEP. It is important to be aware of these.

What Standards Are Appropriate for Classified Students?

In some respects, you really face two tasks when working with included and other classified students, at least from an assessment perspective. On one hand, you want the students to be included in classroom activities as much as possible, and this will include assessments to the degree possible. At the same time, you don't want to frustrate students who face special challenges by giving them assessments on which they have little or no chance for success. So your first task concerns what to give classified students in terms of assessments. Your second task concerns scoring their efforts and translating those scores into grades.

Do Different Assessments Have to Be Developed?

Our recommendation is to make the assessments for classified students the same or as close to the same as possible as the assessments for nonclassified students. If special accommodations have to be made, they should try to maintain the spirit of the original to the degree possible. For example, let's consider a fourth-grade classroom where students are working on (the dreaded) story problems in mathematics. This is an example of such a problem:

The Problem of Harry's Rabbits

Standard Format

> Harry has just gotten back from the grocery store, where he bought 20 carrot sticks for his two rabbits, Pearl and Daisy. He puts 10 carrots into each of their cages. If Pearl eats six of the carrot sticks and Daisy eats half as many as Pearl, how many carrot sticks does Harry have left?

Let's now consider two classified students in this class. Mary is classified as learning disabled. She has problems with reading, in particular, reading comprehension. The trouble Mary is likely to have with this problem is understanding what to do. Jack on the other hand, has somewhat more severe problems with learning than Mary. He will have trouble conceptualizing the problem and maintaining focus on what he is to do all the way through the problem to completion.

As their teacher, what are you to do with a set of problems of this nature? Well, let's begin by specifying when this problem is to be done and under what conditions. There may be 10 problems of this nature to do and the assessment for the classroom in general may be to complete all 10 during a half-hour testing period in the classroom. Let's look at possible adjustments. Mary has trouble with reading comprehension. When we look at the problem carefully, there is a fair amount of extraneous information and verbiage in this question. We might rewrite the question for Mary like this:

The Problem of Harry's Rabbits

Modified Format

> Harry has two rabbits named Pearl and Daisy. He puts 10 carrots into each of their cages. Pearl eats six of her carrot sticks. Daisy eats half as many as Pearl. How many carrot sticks does Harry have left?

The math doesn't change here, nor does the essential nature of trying to restructure the story into what is needed to solve the problem. What has been removed is a substantial portion of the reading comprehension load. This will allow Mary to focus on developing and displaying her math ability free of some of the difficulties she is experiencing in reading comprehension. You may want to modify some of the 10 problems, some substantially and some slightly, in an effort to help Mary develop her reading comprehension skills. As mentioned earlier, the key in working with students who experience exceptional challenges is trying to address their individual needs. We are not expert in the area of special education, and our goal here is to present some of what is possible.

The challenge with Jack is somewhat different than the challenge with Mary. We might want to employ several different ideas with Jack. First, we may want to employ the modified format of the rabbit story. Second, if Jack has professional help in the classroom, we may want to utilize that help in working with Jack on the problems. The aide can provide Jack with just enough help to work the problems, always challenging him to do as much as he can on his own. The aide can keep track of the type of help that was necessary to complete the problem. If might also be the case that Jack will have to complete the assessment at home, with the help of his parents if possible. Finally, Jack may benefit from manipulatives. With 20 sticks to represent the carrots and with containers to represent the cages, Jack can work through the problem physically, which will help him keep track of where he is.

Do Different Scoring Standards Have to Be Used?

When you evaluate the work of these students, you have to differentiate marking work as right or wrong and giving partial credit from what you are going to make of the performance that the student has provided. That is, you mark the paper accurately, but the standards you use for determining anything like a grade has to return to the issue of what the instructional goals are for the student and what this level of performance represents in relationship to those goals.

If, for example, Mary gets three questions correct that were given a modified format, then does fairly well on four problems that had a moderate rewriting, then fairly poorly on three problems that were not rewritten at all—what are you to conclude? Well, it seems like Mary has pretty good control of the math in this regard, but is still having difficulty with the reading. Depending on the exact nature of the situation, you might give her a high mark on her math assignment. For the rest of the students in the class, your instructional goal may be more strongly related to disambiguating the verbal statement of the problem from its mathematical consequences; as a result, the same performance from a nonclassified student would not receive as high a mark as it would for Mary.

Jack probably poses more difficult grading problems than Mary. There may be school policy for providing grades for Jack, or there may be specifications in the IEP. If there is not clear guidance provided, it is best to seek out help on this issue. What you don't want to do is to make decisions on your own, then find out they are in conflict with policy or expectations. For example, Jack's IEP may call for his grades to be based on his level of effort rather than his level of performance. It is always best to get as much information as possible before venturing too far in working with students with substantial learning difficulties.

The purpose of this chapter was to communicate the idea that your instructional goals may be different for students who face learning challenges. If the goals are different, the assessments will almost always be somewhat different as well. You can modify the assessments themselves and provide more help, more time, and manipulatives to assist the student in working on a problem. You should mark right and wrong accurately, but when assigning grades, you need to return to goals—yours, the IEP's, and whoever else's. You should also perhaps seek assistance.

CHAPTER 13

Seamless Integration of Goals, Instruction, and Assessment

You have probably figured out by the number of pages left that we are pretty much at the end of the book. We hope you are feeling better prepared to develop a natural approach to assessment in your classroom. If you are a teacher-in-training, we hope that you have garnered some ideas to help you get started on your own approach to natural classroom assessment. If you are a veteran, we hope we have provided a perspective and some ideas that will help you to examine your practices and perhaps make some modifications and refinements in what you do in the classroom. The basic idea behind our efforts in this book is that assessment should be looked at as a natural extension of classroom instruction. The development of assessments by teachers works best when teachers play from their strengths—when they work from instructional activities directly into assessment activities. We think this results in assessments that provide the most pertinent information for making instructional decisions and for providing instruction to students as they progress through the assessments.

Where Do I Go From Here?

We recommend starting from the top and working down. This would begin with a compilation and reconsideration of what your instructional goals are. Start with what is given you by your school, district, and state. Our thinking here is not to fight against goals that you are required to work with, but to work with them. You can blend in goals of your own as well, and even discuss goals with your students as appropriate.

The next step is to look at how you intend to teach your class. What kinds of activities are you going to use to achieve your goals? Then the assessments for your class can be developed from your instructional goals and the activities that evolve from them. If you want to see what instructional goals might look like in a variety of areas or how they might be incorporated in a district-wide approach, we recommend: American Association for the Advancement of Science (1993), Center for Civic Education (1994), National Council for the Social Studies (1994), National Council of Teachers of Mathematics (1994), National Geographic Research and Exploration (1994), U.S. Department of Education (1995), and Marzano and Kendall (1996).

Using a broad range of assessment formats allows students a variety of opportunities to show what they can do (see Angelo and Cross, 1993, for some great ideas). Each format has strengths and weaknesses; when making your choices among the options, consider the instructional goals you are trying to assess. In developing assessments based on your classroom instruction, be certain to review the assessments from the perspective of the student. Does the student understand clearly what is expected and how the assessment will be evaluated?

In scoring assessments and communicating results, remember (a) that the ultimate goal is instructional and (b) that students need honest and objective information about their levels of achievement in order to grow. When working with students with exceptional needs or challenges, return to the instructional goals that exist for those students and adjust your assessment activities accordingly.

That wraps it up. We hope that you have gotten something worthwhile out of our efforts and that you enjoyed the reading. We wish you the best in your assessment and other instructional activities, and we hope that you continue to grow in this most important of occupations, being a teacher.

References

American Association for the Advancement of Science. (1993). *Benchmarks for science literacy.* New York: Oxford University Press.

Angelo, T., & Cross, K. P. (1993). *Classroom assessment techniques.* San Francisco: Jossey-Bass.

Bloom, B. S., Engelhart, M. D., Frost, E. J., Hill, W. H., & Krathwohl, D. R. (1956). *Taxonomy of educational objectives. Handbook I: Cognitive domain.* New York: David McKay.

Center for Civic Education. (1994). *National standards for civics and government.* Calabasas, CA: Author.

Cizek, G. J. (1999). *Cheating: How to do it, detect it, and prevent it.* Mahwah, NJ: Lawrence Erlbaum.

Danielson, C., & Marquez, E. (1998). *A collection of performance tasks and rubrics: High school mathematics.* Princeton, NJ: Eye on Education.

Dewey, J. (1900). *The child and the curriculum.* Chicago: University of Chicago Press.

Dewey, J. (1916). *Democracy and education.* New York: Free Press.

Dewey, J. (1938). *Experience and education.* New York: Macmillan.

Gallagher, A. M., & De Lisi, R. (1994). Gender differences in Scholastic Aptitude Test—Mathematics problem solving among high-ability students. *Journal of Educational Psychology, 86,* 204-211.

Glatthorn, A. A. (1998). *Performance assessment and standards-based curricula: The achievement cycle.* Princeton, NJ: Eye on Education.

Goodrich, H. (1996). Understanding rubrics. *Educational Leadership, 54,*(4), 14-17.

Guskey, T. R. (1994). *High stakes performance assessment: Perspectives on Kentucky's education reform.* Thousand Oaks, CA: Corwin.

Haladyna, T. M. (1994). *Developing and validating multiple-choice test items.* Hillsdale, NJ: Lawrence Erlbaum.

Haladyna, T. M. (1997). *Writing test items to evaluate higher order thinking.* Boston: Allyn & Bacon.

Hill, B. C., & Ruptic, C. A. (1994). *Practical aspects of authentic assessment.* Norwood, MA: Christopher Gordon.

Johnson, B. (1996a). *The performance assessment handbook: Vol. 1. Portfolios and Socratic seminars.* Princeton, NJ: Eye on Education.

Johnson, B. (1996b). *The performance assessment handbook: Vol. 2. Performances and exhibitions.* Princeton, NJ: Eye on Education.

Linn, R., Baker, E., & Dunbar, S. (1991). Complex, performance-based assessment: Expectations and validation criteria. *Educational Researcher, 20,* 15-21.

Marzano, R. J., & Kendall, J. S. (1996). *A comprehensive guide to designing standards-based districts, schools, and classrooms.* Alexandria, VA: Association for Supervision and Curriculum Development.

Messick, S. (1989). Validity. In R. L. Linn (Ed.), *Educational measurement* (3rd ed.). New York: Macmillan.

Morrow, L. M., & Smith, J. K. (1990). The effects of group size on children's comprehension of oral stories. *Reading Research Quarterly, 25*(3), 213-231.

National Council for the Social Studies. (1994). *Curriculum standards for social studies: Expectations of excellence.* Washington, DC: Author.

National Council of Teachers of Mathematics. (1994). *Professional standards for school mathematics.* Reston, VA: Author.

National Geographic Research and Exploration. (1994). *Geography for life: National geography standards.* Washington, DC: Author.

Nitko, A. J. (1989). Designing tests that are integrated with instruction. In R. L. Linn (Ed.), *Educational Measurement* (3rd ed., pp. 447-474). New York: Macmillan.

Ohio State Department of Education. (1999). *Ohio proficiency tests: Learning outcomes.* Columbus, OH: Author.

Rhodes, L. K. (1993). *Literacy assessment: A handbook of instruments.* Portsmouth, NH: Heinemann Educational Books.

Scriven, M. (1967). The methodology of evaluation. *AERA Monograph Series on Curriculum Evaluation, 1,* 39-83.

Shavelson, R. J., Baxter, G. P., & Pine, J. (1991). Performance assessment in science. *Applied Measurement in Education, 4,* 347-362.

Smith, J. K. (1980). *The role of measurement in the process of instruction* (ERIC TM Report No. 70.) Princeton, NJ: Educational Testing Service.

Stiggins, R. (1991). *Student-centered classroom assessment.* New York: Macmillan.

U.S. Department of Education. (1995). *Teachers and goals 2000: Leading the journey toward high standards for all teachers.* Washington, DC: Author.

Van der Veer, R., & Valsiner, J. (1994). *The Vygotsky reader.* Oxford, UK: Blackwell.

Vermont State Department of Education. (1999). *History and social sciences standards, reasoning and problem solving standards.* Montpelier, VT: Author.

Vygotsky, L. S. (1978). *Mind in society: The development of higher mental processes.* Cambridge, MA: Harvard University Press.

Wiggins, G. (1996). Practicing what we preach in designing authentic assessments? *Educational Leadership, 54*(4), 18-25.

Wolf, L. F., & Smith, J. K. (1995). The consequence of consequence: Motivation, anxiety, and test performance. *Applied Measurement in Education, 8,* 227-242.

Wolf, L. F., Smith, J. K., & Birnbaum, M. E. (1995). Consequences of performance, test motivation, and mentally taxing items. *Applied Measurement in Education, 8,* 341-352.

Index

CORWIN
PRESS

The Corwin Press logo—a raven striding across an open book—represents the happy union of courage and learning. We are a professional-level publisher of books and journals for K–12 educators, and we are committed to creating and providing resources that embody these qualities. Corwin's motto is "Success for All Learners."